EVERTON
THE ULTIMATE BOOK OF STATS AND FACTS

© Dave Ball and Gavin Buckland 2001

Published by The Bluecoat Press, Liverpool
Book design by March Design, Liverpool
Printed by Biddles

Front cover
Dixie Dean in action 1934

ISBN 1 872568 79 3

EVERTON
THE ULTIMATE BOOK OF STATS AND FACTS

Dave Ball and Gavin Buckland

The Bluecoat Press

CONTENTS

INTRODUCTION

Although there have been several books published which have chronicled the fortunes of Everton, there has never been a book which has concentrated solely on the facts and trivia associated with one of this country's most successful clubs.

The aims of the book are not only to provide the answers to several questions but, both being sports quiz addicts, to provide the basis for some interesting questions at the next game. So, for the first time you will be able to find out the answers to such questions as: Dixie Dean is amongst the most prolific forwards in history – but which 2 players had a better scoring record for the club? Why is Kevin Richardson unique amongst all the players who have appeared in English football? Who scored at both ends against Watford in 1984, and did the same against the same club 2 years later? How does Harry Catterick compare with the other managerial greats of the 1960s? [Answer: rather well as it happens.] How did Danny Cadamarteri make Everton history against Leicester City in February 2001?

Also included, and we believe this is for the first time in any publication about any club, are the playing and goal-scoring records of League clubs against Everton. So, if you have had sleepless nights wondering who is Hull City's record scorer against the Blues, the answer is here.

Obviously, for a book of this nature there are several unanswered questions, which we aim to tackle in future editions if possible. Not least amongst these are the christian names of several players from the early days and the instances [before 1970], of penalties and players sent off. If any readers can assist us in these areas, then a note to the publishers would be appreciated.

Many publications have been referenced in putting this book together, but a special mention must go to those monuments to footballing statistics, *Rothman's Football Yearbooks*, *Hugman's Football League Players Records* and various Association of Football Statisticians publications. Also, John Keith's and Peter Thomas's *A-Z of Mersey Soccer* and John Robert's *Centenary History* were invaluable in looking at the early history of the club.

Status of games

One of the main issues surrounding football statistics is the status of games, namely what should be regarded as 'first class' and what should not?

Unlike cricket, in which the status of matches is formulated by the authorities, there is no definitive guide in football; grey areas still surround the status of games such as the Charity Shield, Screen Sport Super Cup etc.

To that end, it has been decided that 'first class' games for Everton, unless specifically mentioned, should be classed as those for which there is universal agreement: namely the 3 major domestic competitions [League, FA Cup and League Cup] and the 3 European competitions [European Cup, European Cup Winners' Cup and the Fairs/UEFA Cup].

FOREWORD

Have you ever wondered what keeps sportsmen occupied when they are not actually involved in playing their own sport? Well, many of us watch television, play cards and do crosswords, whilst a number of us participate in sports quizzes. While I do not presume to be a mastermind, I do try to keep up with a number of sports because of my commitment to BBC TV's *A Question of Sport*, but I admit that I do have a real attachment to Everton Football Club.

My first experience of the Goodison 'roar' was a victory over Manchester United, when George Best was at his peak. I was only a youngster then, so I missed the halcyon days of Harry Catterick, but I feel privileged to say that I witnessed the great era of the 1980s, when so many great players paraded their skills at Goodison.

I have known Dave Ball for a number of years, as he is the longest serving member of the production team on *Question of Sport*. He is a former BBC *Brain of Sport*, he writes for the *Liverpool Echo* and set the questions of ITV's *Sportsmasters*, with Dickie Davies and was a researcher in the early days of BSB and BskyB.

Dave's co-author, Gavin Buckland, also works on *A Question of Sport* and, like Dave, is a member of Radio Merseyside's Sports Team and a researcher for Granada TV. Gavin has been the Merseyside Sports Quiz Champion for the past decade, his passion for Everton goes back to the 1970s and his particular favourite was Bob Latchford.

Both Dave and Gavin are experts in other sports; they also set the questions for Transworld International's Cricket Quiz, which was syndicated worldwide.
Between them, they have spent hours researching the past glories and failures of the club. This is a book full of facts, trivia and recollections, but if you are the quiz 'type', both playing and compiling, then this book is a must. I hope that you will enjoy the book as much as I will, because it will be a constant companion when I am cooped up in a hotel room, in places such as Dubai, Deauville or Derby.

John Parrott

HONOURS AND TITLES

Honours and titles

- Everton have won 15 major honours: 9 League titles, 5 FA Cups and 1 European Cup Winners' Cup.

- Everton have been League champions on 9 occasions – in 1891, 1915, 1928, 1932, 1939, 1963, 1970, 1985 and 1987. Only Liverpool, Manchester United and Arsenal have exceeded this total.

- The Blues won the League title in the seasons prior to both World Wars.

- In 1984-85 Everton won the League title by a then record margin of 13 points – despite losing their first 2 matches and then 3 of the last 4 games, due to a combination of international call-ups and rested players.

- In 1984-85, Everton became the only English side to win the League title and the European Cup Winners' Cup in the same season.

- In the same season, the Blues became only the 2nd team [after Liverpool in 1977] to win the League title and also appear in an FA Cup and European Final in the same season. They remain the only side ever to go into the FA Cup Final having won 2 trophies in the season.

- Everton were rightly voted European Team of the Year in 1985.

- Between 1930-31 and 1932-33, Everton became the first English side to win the 2nd Division, 1st Division and FA Cup in successive seasons.

- In 1985-86 Everton became only the 3rd post-War side to be runners-up in both the League and FA Cup in the same season – after Burnley [1962], Leeds United [1965 and 1970]. They have since been joined by Manchester United in 1995 and Arsenal in 2001.

- Everton are one of only 10 clubs who have never slipped below the top 2 divisions. The other 9 are Arsenal, Chelsea, Leeds United, Leicester City, Liverpool, Manchester United, Newcastle United, Tottenham Hotspur and West Ham United.

- Only Arsenal have exceeded Everton's current tenure in the English top-flight.

Players' medals

- Neville Southall is the only Everton player to have won 5 major medals with the club. His collection consists of 2 League Championship medals [1985 and 1987], 2 FA Cup medals [1984 and 1995] and one European Cup Winners' Cup medal.

- The following players won 4 medals [2 League titles, 1 FA Cup and Cup Winners' Cup medal] between 1984 and 1987: Alan Harper, Derek Mountfield, Kevin Ratcliffe, Peter Reid, Graeme Sharp, Trevor Steven and Gary Stevens.

- Kevin Ratcliffe is the club's most successful captain, lifting 4 trophies in his time as skipper.

- No player has won 3 League titles with the club, but 3 players – Warney Cresswell, Ted Critchley and Dixie Dean – won two 1st Division titles in 1928 and 1932, plus the 2nd Division title in 1931. Jock Thomson was the only player to win medals in the League Championship in 1932 and 1939, plus the 2nd Division title in 1931.

- In the post-War era, Kevin Richardson [Everton 1985 and Arsenal 1989] and Bobby Mimms [Everton 1987 and Blackburn 1995] have won League Championship medals with the Blues and another club.

- Kevin Richardson holds a unique place in English football, as the only player to have won the 3 major domestic trophies with different clubs: League [Arsenal 1989], FA Cup [Everton 1984] and League Cup [Aston Villa 1994].

- Trevor Steven is one of the most decorated players in British football history, winning 2 League titles with Everton, 5 with Rangers and a French League title with Marseille in 1992. He also won the FA Cup with Everton in 1984 and 4 Scottish League Cups with Rangers.

Medals in England and Scotland

Players who won a League Championship medal with Everton and also a Championship medal in Scotland.

Dan Doyle	Everton title winner in 1891 and Scottish Championship with Celtic
James Gault	1915, Rangers
Torry Gillick	1939, Rangers
Alex Stevenson	1939, Rangers
Alex Scott	1963, Rangers
George Thomson and Alex Young	1963, Hearts
Gary Stevens and Trevor Steven	1985 and 1987, Rangers
Andy Gray	1985, Rangers

Players' honours

- Gary Lineker is the only Everton player to have won both the major Footballer of the Year awards – the PFA and Football Writers' – in the same year [1986].

- Peter Reid won the PFA Player of the Year award in 1985 and was followed by Neville Southall as the Football Writers' choice in the same year.

- Several other Everton players have won either of the 2 major awards with another club. Most notably Andy Gray, who is the only player to have won the PFA Young Player and Player of the Year Awards in the same year [whilst with Aston Villa in 1977].

Olympic winners

- Harold Hardman played for the victorious Great Britain team at the 1908 Olympics, and Daniel Amokachi won an Olympic Gold medal with Nigeria in the 1996 Atlanta Games shortly after leaving Everton.

Honours at other sports

- Harry Makepeace, who played for the club from 1903 to 1915, holds a unique record as the only man to win: FA Cup Winners medal – Everton 1906; League Championship medal – Everton 1915; 4 international football caps for England from 1906 – 1912; County Cricket Championship medal – Lancashire 1926, 1927, 1928 and 1930; International cricket caps – 4 England v Australia 1920-21 [including 117 at Melbourne].

- Jack Sharp [1899 – 1910] has a very similar record, playing both football [2 caps] and cricket [3 caps] for England. He scored a test century at the Oval in 1909 against Australia and also captained Lancashire. He also won an FA Cup Winners' medal with Everton in 1906.

- Benjamin Baker, who played in goal for Everton in the early 1920s, competed in the high jump for Britain in the 1912 and 1920 Olympics [finishing 6th] and also held the British record for the event. He played both amateur and professional football for England and also played cricket for Liverpool.

THE LEAGUE CHAMPIONSHIP

1890-91 WINNERS

- Everton win the title by 2 points from Preston – the full record being P22 W14 D1 L7 PTS 29.

- Leading goalscorer is Fred Geary, with 20 League goals.

- Ever-presents are Edgar Chadwick, Fred Geary, and Alfred Milward.

- Preston are the only side Everton fail to beat in either of their League matches during the season.

- Title season started with 5 consecutive victories, during which 23 goals are scored and just 2 conceded.

1914-15 WINNERS

- The Blues win the title by a single point from Oldham Athletic, after drawing the final League match against Chelsea, while Oldham lost against Liverpool – the full record is P38 W19 D8 L11 PTS 46. Just 3 points separate the first 7 teams.

- Leading goalscorer is Bobby Parker, with 36 League goals.

- No player is ever-present for the 38 League matches – highest are Joe Clennell and Tom Fern with 36 games each.

- Everton fail to beat 5 of the 18 other sides in the Division in either of their League matches – Burnley, Middlesbrough, Sheffield United, Oldham and Blackburn.

- A strange end to the season sees Everton win 2 and lose 4 of their last 8 home games and win 6 out of their last 7 away matches. For the first time ever – since matched in 1957-58 and 1992-93 – the Blues win more matches away [11] than at home [8] in a season.

1927-28 WINNERS

- Everton clinch the title by 2 points from Huddersfield – the full record is P42 W20 D13 L9 PTS 53.

- The season is memorable for Dixie Dean's record 60 League goals.

- Ever-presents are full-back Jack O'Donnell and Alec Troup.

- Dick Forshaw becomes the first – and so far only player – to win title honours with both Everton and Liverpool, having won the title with the latter club in 1922-23.

- The season was characterised by a strange set of League results: Everton's 20 League wins are against 17 different sides and they win home and away against just 3 teams: Aston Villa, Burnley and Sheffield Wednesday. Everton fail to win any of the 9 League matches from 21 January to 24 March.

- Arsenal, Bolton, Huddersfield and Liverpool are unbeaten against the Blues in League games.

1931-32 WINNERS

- The Blues win the title by 2 points from Arsenal – P42 W26 D 4 L12 PTS 56.
- The 116 League goals scored are a record for the club in the top-flight. Top scorer is Dean with 45 goals in 38 games.
- Everton fail to beat Manchester City and Arsenal in either of their League matches against those clubs.
- No player is ever-present, although Ted Sagar and Tommy Johnson each play in 41 matches.

1938-39 WINNERS

- Everton win the title from Wolves by 4 points – P42 W27 D5 L10 PTS 59.
- The Blues set new club records for wins and points in the top-flight.
- Runners-up, Wolves, defeat the Blues 7-0 in a League match on 22 February, as well as knocking them out of the FA Cup, 2-0 at Molineux in the 6th Round.
- Norman 'Rollicker' Greenhalgh – the one full-back feared by Sir Stanley Matthews – is the only ever-present.
- Top scorer is Tommy Lawton with 34 goals in 38 matches. He scored in the first 6 League games of the season, a record that has not been matched since.
- The following sides are unbeaten in League matches against the Blues: Charlton, Derby County and Stoke City.

1962-63 WINNERS

- Everton win the title by 6 points from Spurs in the year of the 'big freeze': P42 W25 D11 D6 PTS 61.
- The Blues are unbeaten in their last 12 matches – winning 8 and drawing 4.
- Top scorer is Roy Vernon, with 24 goals in 41 matches.
- Only ever-presents are Dennis Stevens and Alex Young.
- Everton fail to defeat Arsenal, Blackburn and Liverpool in League matches.

1969-70 WINNERS

- The Blues enjoy their finest ever season in the top-flight, winning the title with 66 points and by 9 points from Leeds – P42 W29 D8 L5 PTS 66.
- Everton achieve the rare feat of defeating all other 21 clubs in the Division during the season.
- The first 18 matches see 15 wins and 2 draws and just one defeat – at Derby. Eight consecutive games were won from 7 March onwards.
- Top scorer is Joe Royle with 23 goals in 42 matches. Other ever-presents are Gordon West, Tommy Wright and John Hurst.

1984-85 WINNERS

- Everton win the title by a record 13 points [3 points for a win] from Liverpool – P42 W28 D6 L8 PTS 90.

- The Blues again defeat all other 21 clubs in the division – the first instance since Everton in 1970.

- The Blues hit the top for the first time on 3 November, after defeating Leicester 3-0 at Goodison, the first time Everton top the table since 1979.

- Strangely, in such a successful season, Everton concede 4 goals in 5 different League games: Tottenham, Watford, Norwich, Chelsea and Coventry.

- Graeme Sharp is top scorer with 21 goals. No player scores a hat trick, although 8 players score 2 goals in a game. Five players get into double figures: Sharp, Steven, Sheedy, Heath and Mountfield.

- Only Neville Southall is ever-present.

- Only one game is goalless – at Queens Park Rangers on 8 December 1984.

1986-87 WINNERS

- Everton reverse the placings from the previous year by pushing Liverpool into second place – P42 W26 D8 L8 PTS 86 – the same record as 12 months previously.

- The Blues win the title thanks to 2 major offensives over Christmas and Easter – 6 consecutive wins from 20 December – 17 January, and 7 consecutive wins from 14 March – 20 April.

- Top-scorer is Trevor Steven, with 14 goals in 41 games, although Kevin Sheedy's 13 goals in 28 games is statistically superior. Wayne Clarke against Newcastle is the only hat trick scorer.

- Only Kevin Ratcliffe is ever-present.

- Only Liverpool deprive Everton of matching their achievement of 1970 and 1985 in defeating all other 21 clubs in League games during the season.

Comparison of League Championship-winning seasons

The following table compares the Blues' 9 Championship-winning seasons, the benchmark being the percentage of available points actually won, [using 2 points for a win].

	P	W	D	L	F	A	Points	Max	%
1969-70	42	29	8	5	72	34	66	84	79%
1984-85	42	28	6	8	88	43	62	84	74%
1962-63	42	25	11	6	84	42	61	84	73%
1986-87	42	26	8	8	76	31	60	84	71%
1938-39	42	27	5	10	88	52	59	84	70%
1931-32	42	26	4	12	116	64	56	84	67%
1890-91	22	14	1	7	63	29	29	44	66%
1927-28	42	20	13	9	102	66	53	84	63%
1914-15	38	19	8	11	76	47	46	76	61%

- As you can see, 1969-70 is clearly the best season in the club's history, with the team winning 79% of the points available.

- The other noticeable point is that the records near the bottom of this table can be significantly inferior to some other seasons when the title was not won. For example, 2nd place in 1985-86 saw 71% of the points available won, and a superior goal difference puts it ahead of 1986-87, to rank as the 4th best season in the top-flight.

The top 10 seasons in the top-flight

These make interesting reading, using the same methodology.

	P	W	D	L	F	A	Points	Max	%	Position
1969-70	42	29	8	5	72	34	66	84	79%	1st
1984-85	42	28	6	8	88	43	62	84	74%	1st
1962-63	42	25	11	6	84	42	61	84	73%	1st
1985-86	42	26	8	8	87	41	60	84	71%	2nd
1986-87	42	26	8	8	76	31	60	84	71%	1st
1889-90	22	14	3	5	65	40	31	44	70%	2nd
1938-39	42	27	5	10	88	52	59	84	70%	1st
1894-95	30	18	6	6	82	50	42	60	70%	2nd
1904-05	34	21	5	8	63	36	47	68	69%	2nd
1968-69	42	21	15	6	77	36	57	84	68%	3rd

- 4 League Championship years are therefore not part of the Blues 10 best seasons, in terms of the percentage of points won. On this comparison, 1931-32 is 11th, 1890-91 is 12th, 1927-28 is 17th and 1914-15 is 24th on the list!

- 1968-69 was a particularly good performance, as 57 points was for 3rd place, behind Leeds [67] and Liverpool [61]. This equalled Wolves' record for the highest number of points scored by a team finishing 3rd in the League, and is a better performance than 15 title-winning sides since World War I.

10 worst seasons in the top-flight

Four of the club's 10 worst seasons have been in the past 8 years. Again calculated using 2 points for a win.

	P	W	D	L	F	A	Points	Max	%	Position
1996-97	38	10	12	16	44	57	32	76	42%	15th
1979-80	42	9	17	16	43	51	35	84	42%	19th
1929-30	42	12	11	19	80	92	35	84	42%	22nd
1924-25	42	12	11	19	40	60	35	84	42%	17th
2000-01	38	11	9	18	45	59	31	76	41%	16th
1997-98	38	9	13	16	41	56	31	76	41%	17th
1949-50	42	10	14	18	42	66	34	84	40%	18th
1926-27	42	12	10	20	64	90	34	84	40%	20th
1993-94	42	12	8	22	42	63	32	84	38%	17th
1950-51	42	12	8	22	48	86	32	84	38%	22th

Decade by decade comparison of League performance

The following table gives a decade-by-decade comparison of the Blues' League performance by averaging out their results over 10 year cycles, converting all results to a 42-game season – the 1960s, for example, consists of the 10 seasons from 1960-61 – 1969-70 inclusive. An average League position for each decade is given.

	W	D	L	F	A	Points	Position
1960s	21	10	11	75	51	52	4th
1980s	20	10	12	65	44	50	6th
1890s	21	7	14	90	68	49	5th
1900s	20	7	15	71	56	47	6th
1930s	19	9	14	90	72	47	12th
1910s	17	10	15	61	55	44	8th
1970s	14	14	14	53	51	42	10th
1920s	15	11	16	67	68	41	13th
1950s	15	10	17	66	73	40	20th
1990s	13	13	16	52	55	39	13th
1940s	14	10	18	49	66	38	15th

- The 1960s was the club's most sustained period of consistency in their League history. Only once during the decade were Everton out of the top 10 [11th in the Cup-winning year of 1965-66] and their average League position of 4th was the highest of any club during the decade, ahead of Spurs, whose average League position was 5th.

- The League position for seasons outside the top-flight was calculated by using 1st place in Division 2 as 23rd in the League etc.

- The 1990s was the club's worst period in a full 10-year cycle – as the 1940s consisted of just 4 seasons, due to World War II.

EVERTON IN THE FA CUP

FA Cup victories

Everton have won the FA Cup 5 times.

1906	1-0	Newcastle
1933	3-0	Manchester City
1966	3-2	Sheffield Wednesday
1984	2-0	Watford
1995	1-0	Manchester United

Losing finalists

In addition, the Blues have lost in the Final on 7 occasions.

1893	0-1	Wolverhampton Wanderers
1897	2-3	Aston Villa
1907	1-2	Sheffield Wednesday
1968	0-1	West Bromwich Albion
1985	0-1	Manchester United
1986	1-3	Liverpool
1989	2-3	Liverpool

- In 1986, Everton became only the 5th team [and only the 2nd at Wembley after Arsenal 1978 – 1980] to appear in 3 consecutive FA Cup Finals. Their consecutive defeats in 1985 and 1986 were only the 2nd such instance in Wembley history, after Manchester United in 1957 and 1958.

- Kevin Ratcliffe, Graeme Sharp, Trevor Steven [1984 – 1985 –1986 – 1989] and Neville Southall [1984 – 1985 – 1989 – 1995] are the only players to have appeared in 4 FA Cup Finals for the Blues.

- Jack Taylor [1897 – 1906 – 1907] was the first player to appear in 3 FA Cup Finals for the club.

- Kevin Sheedy, Paul Bracewell and Pat Van Den Hauwe [1985 – 1986 – 1989] are the only players to appear in 3 FA Cup Finals for the Blues without gaining a winner's medal.

1906 FA CUP WINNERS

● Everton win their 1st FA Cup Final, at the 3rd time of asking, with a 1-0 win over Newcastle United. Their Semi Final victory over Liverpool taking place at Villa Park of all places!

● Everton reached the Final with the help of a home draw in every round, strangely this had also happened in their only 2 previous trips to the Final.

1933 FA CUP WINNERS

● Everton win the FA Cup for a second time in the year when numbered shirts were worn for the first time, with the Blues being allocated 1 – 11 and their opponents 12 – 22.

● Tommy Johnson becomes the first player to gain a winner's medal against a previous club he had played for in a Wembley FA Cup Final, having appeared with Manchester City in 1926.

● Albert Geldard [19 years and 18 days] and Warney Cresswell [38 years and 175 days] set records for the Blues' youngest and oldest players in Wembley FA Cup Finals, which still stand today.

1966 FA CUP WINNERS

● Everton storm to the Final without conceding a goal in their 7 matches, the first side to achieve this since 1903.

● They become the first side to win the FA Cup Final from 2-0 down.

● Cup Final hero, Mike Trebilcock, a controversial replacement for Fred Pickering, scores twice having played in just 7 League games for the club. Only one player in the post-War era [Arthur Turner of Charlton, who made his debut in the 1946 Final] had made fewer appearances for his club prior to an FA Cup Final, at the time.

● Mike Trebilcock remains the Blues' youngest Cup Final scorer at Wembley, at 21 years 166 days.

● Sheffield Wednesday's Don Megson was the father of future Everton mid-fielder, Gary Megson.

● Everton win the Cup having finished 11th in the League, which coincidentally had been their final League placing in 1906 and 1933.

1984 FA CUP WINNERS

- Everton win the FA Cup after conceding just one goal, to Notts County's John Chiedozie, in 8 matches.

- John Barnes makes the first of his 2 appearances against Everton in FA Cup Finals, the only player to do so with different sides [Watford and Liverpool].

- Everton match the feat of Tottenham and Manchester United in the 2 previous years of winning the FA Cup, after losing the League Cup Final to Liverpool earlier in the season.

- The Blues namesakes, Everton of Chile, make it a double by winning the Chilean FA Cup.

1995 FA CUP WINNERS

- Like 1984, Everton win the trophy having conceded just one goal, a penalty by Jurgen Klinsmann of Spurs in the Semi Final. This means that in their last 3 Cup-winning campaigns [1966, 1984 and 1995] the Blues had played a total of 19 matches in reaching Wembley, and conceded just 2 goals.

- Neville Southall [1984 and 1995] becomes the first player to win 2 winners' medals with Everton. Only he and Mark Hughes are the survivors from the 1985 Final between the 2 sides.

- Duncan Ferguson makes the first of his 2 substitute appearances in the Final [he would come on for Newcastle against Manchester United in 1999], the only player to do so for different sides.

- Gary Ablett sets several records as a result of his appearance for Everton.
  • The first player to gain FA Cup winner's medals with with both Everton and Liverpool. • The first player to appear both for and against Everton in FA Cup Finals [his other medal was won with Liverpool in 1989]. • In all, he was the 7th player to appear against Everton in Wembley Finals and also play for the Blues.

FA Cup trivia

- In the 1906 Final, Everton fielded a Scott, Alex Young and a Sharp. In the 1966 Final, they fielded a Scott and Alex Young again and in 1984 another Sharp! Indeed the Alex Youngs of the victorious 1906 and 1966 sides provide the only instance of namesakes gaining winners' medals with the same club in FA Cup history.

- Harold Hardman, in 1906 and 1907, was the only amateur to appear in 2 FA Cup Finals in the 20th century.

- Stuart McCall made Cup Final history in 1989, by becoming the first substitute to score twice in an FA Cup Final – a feat then matched by Ian Rush in the same game.

- Everton's 1933 Final scorer Jimmy Dunn and his son, Jimmy [with Wolves in 1949], provided the first instance of a father and son gaining winners' medals at Wembley.

- Only one set of brothers, William and Robert Balmer, have played in FA Cup Finals for Everton; both played in the 1907 Final against Sheffield Wednesday, with William also playing in the 1906 Final.

- In 1995, Dave Watson matched Emlyn Hughes' feat of lifting the FA Cup and League Cup at Wembley with different clubs. Watson had captained Norwich City to victory in the 1985 League Cup Final.

- Kevin Ratcliffe [1984 – 1985 – 1986 – 1989] is the only player to captain a side in 4 FA Cup Finals at Wembley.

- Tommy Johnson [v Manchester City, 1933] and Kevin Sheedy [v Liverpool 1986 – 1989] are the only Everton players to appear in FA Cup Finals at Wembley against former clubs.

- Derek Mountfield was the only player in the 1985 Final against Manchester United not to win an international cap in his career.

- Only 2 players have appeared in Wembley FA Cup Finals for Everton with the same surname – Ray Wilson in 1966 and Ian Wilson [sub] in 1989.

- Everton lost the 1968 FA Cup to West Bromwich Albion, having won 6-2 at the Hawthorns just 2 months prior to the Final, Alan Ball scoring 4 times.

- Wimbledon ended Everton's quest for 4 consecutive FA Cup Final appearances in 1986-87, and also stopped the next side to appear in 3 consecutive Finals – Manchester United – from making it 4, in 1996-97. Coincidentally, Everton had stopped Arsenal from reaching 4 consecutive Finals in 1980-81.

The draw

- Everton's most common opponents in the FA Cup are Liverpool [P20, W6 D5 L9] and Sheffield Wednesday [P19, W9 D5 L5]. These are also the 2 most played fixtures in FA Cup history.

- Everton have not been drawn against the same team in 3 consecutive seasons. The nearest was playing Liverpool 3 times in 4 seasons in the 1980s [1985-86, 1987-88 and 1988-89].

- Discounting the tie against Bolton in 1887-88, from which Everton were disqualified over player eligibility, the Blues played just one FA Cup tie which went to a 3rd replay: the 4-game saga against Sheffield Wednesday, in the 1987-88 3rd Round. The tie was memorably settled by a 5-0 first half burst in the 4th match at Hillsborough, where, coincidentally, the Blues, in a League game, had thrown away a 5-goal first half lead in 1904 [result 5-5].

- The Everton-Liverpool 5th Round tie, in 1990-91, created FA Cup history, as it was the last tie in the competition to go to a 2nd replay [Everton winning 1-0] before they were scrapped in favour of penalty shoot-outs the following season. Dave Watson's goal will thus go down in history as the last scored in a 2nd replay.

- It is believed that Everton's feat in coming from behind 4 times in the famous 4-4 draw, in the first replay, is the only such occurrence in English football.

For and against

Players who have appeared against Everton in Wembley FA Cup Finals and have also played for the Blues.

Maurice Johnstone	Watford	1984
John Gidman	Manchester United	1985
Norman Whiteside	Manchester United	1985
Mark Hughes	Manchester United	1985
Steve McMahon	Liverpool	1989
Peter Beardsley	Liverpool	1989
Gary Ablett	Liverpool	1989

FA Cup Semi Finals

Everton have played in a record 23 FA Cup Semi Finals, and a total of 29 games, including replays. The Semi Final record at each ground is shown below.

	P	W	D	L	F	A
Villa Park	7	4	1	2	8	6
Old Trafford	4	1	0	3	2	6
Maine Road	4	0	1	3	5	11
Elland Road	3	1	1	1	5	3
Burnden Park	2	2	0	0	3	1
Molineux	2	1	0	1	3	4
Victoria Ground	2	1	1	0	4	3
Trent Bridge	2	1	0	1	3	3
Bramall Lane	1	0	1	0	2	2
Ewood Park	1	0	1	0	0	0
Highbury	1	1	0	0	1	0
Totals	29	12	6	11	36	39

- Liverpool are the Blues' most frequent opponents, being drawn together 4 times at this stage [1906, 1950, 1971 and 1977]. The only other sides to face Everton on more than one occasion are Derby County [1896 and 1897], West Bromwich Albion [1907 and 1931] and West Ham [1933 and 1980].

- Only 2 players have scored twice in a Semi Final: John W Parker [Bolton, 1953] and Daniel Amokachi [Spurs, 1995].

- Edgar Chadwick is the only player to have scored in Semi Finals in 3 different seasons, doing so against Preston in 1893 and Derby County in 1897 and 1898.

- Jack Taylor [1897-98, 1905 – 1907 and 1910] is the only Everton player to appear in 6 Semi Finals. The next highest is Kevin Ratcliffe, with 5 appearances [1980, 1984 – 1986 and 1989].

- Although Everton have played only 4 seasons outside the top-flight, during that time they reached 2 Semi Finals: West Brom [1931] and Bolton [1953]. Although both were lost, the latter was famous for a stirring comeback to 4-3 from 4 goals down. A draw could have been achieved, had Tommy Clinton not missed a penalty.

- Brian Kidd became only the 3rd player to be sent off in Semi Final history, when receiving his marching orders in the 1-1 draw against West Ham, at Villa Park, in 1980.

- The last player to score from the penalty spot for the Blues in a Semi Final was Brian Kidd, against West Ham United, in the above game.

- The only substitutes to score for Everton in Semi Finals are Alan Harper [Sheffield Wednesday, 1986] and Daniel Amokachi [Tottenham Hotspur, 1995].

- In the 1980s, Martin Hodge kept goal both for and against Everton in FA Cup Semi Finals – for the Blues against West Ham in 1980 and for Sheffield Wednesday against Everton in 1986.

Everton's biggest victories in the FA Cup

11-2	Derby County [h]	18 January 1890
9-1	Southport [h]	28 February 1931
8-0	Doncaster Rovers [h]	21 January 1939

- The biggest post-War victories are 5-0 against Colchester [1970-71], Sheffield Wednesday [1987-88] and Norwich City [1994-95].
- The Blues' biggest away victory in the Cup is against Crystal Palace [6-0] in 1930-31, the biggest away win post-War being Sheffield Wednesday [above].

Everton's biggest defeats in the FA Cup

0-6	Crystal Palace [h]	7 January 1922
0-5	Derby County [a]	25 February 1911

- The biggest post-War defeat was the 4-0 loss to Liverpool, on 29 January 1955. The 4-1 defeat in a Quarter Final tie against Newcastle, in 1998-99, was the Blues' heaviest Cup defeat since going down 4-1 to Aston Villa in 1958-59.

Unbeaten runs in the FA Cup
The Blues' longest unbeaten runs in the FA Cup are: 14 matches from the 1983-84, 3rd Round win at Stoke, to the Semi Final win against Luton in 1984-85, and 13 matches from the start of the 1905-06 competition.

FA Cup opponents
- Everton have never gone out at the first hurdle in the FA Cup in 3 consecutive seasons. They have lost, however, 3 consecutive FA Cup ties in seasons 1890-91, 1891-92, 1958-59 and 1960-61.
- 3 teams have knocked Everton out of the Cup in consecutive seasons: Sheffield Wednesday [1894-95, 1895-96], Liverpool [1987-88, 1988-89], Newcastle United [1997-98, 1998-99]. Ian Rush scored the winning goals for Liverpool in 1988-89 and Newcastle United in 1997-98.
- Everton have achieved a club record 9 FA Cup victories against Sheffield Wednesday and 8 against Derby County. Liverpool have knocked the Blues out of the Cup on most occasions, doing so 9 times. Everton's favourite Cup opponents are Ipswich Town, whom they have beaten on all 5 occasions when they have been drawn together.
- Everton have gone out to lower Division clubs on 19 occasions in the FA Cup since the War. The only instance of a club from 2 divisions lower winning a tie, was Bradford City [then a 3rd Division side] in their 3-0 win in 1959-60.

Victors from lower divisions

The following clubs have all knocked Everton out of the FA Cup on two occasions, since the War, when in a lower division.

Fulham	1947-48, 1974-75
Bradford City	1959-60, 1996-97
Sheffield United	1960-61, 1969-70
Sunderland	1963-64, 1978-79
West Ham United	1979-80, 1990-91

Non-League opponents since the War

Kings Lynn [h]	1961-62	Won 4-0
Bedford [a]	1965-66	Won 3-0
Altrincham [h]	1974-75	Drew 1-1 [Won replay 2-0]
Telford [h]	1984-85	Won 3-0
Woking [h]	1990-91	Won 1-0

Most goals

Everton's top 10 goalscorers in the history of the FA Cup.

Dixie Dean	1925 – 1937	28 goals	32 games
Graeme Sharp	1980 – 1991	20 goals	54 games
Dave Hickson	1951 – 1959	16 goals	18 games
Kevin Sheedy	1982 – 1992	15 goals	38 games
Alex Young	1901 – 1911	15 goals	39 games
Jack Taylor	1896 – 1910	14 goals	56 games
Edgar Chadwick	1888 – 1899	13 goals	30 games
Jimmy Settle	1899 – 1908	13 goals	32 games
Jack Sharp	1899 – 1910	12 goals	42 games
Tom Browell	1911 – 1913	11 goals	10 games

- Dixie Dean, with 9 goals in 1930-31, holds the record for most goals scored by an Everton player in a single FA Cup campaign. The post-War record is held by Graeme Sharp, with 6 goals in 1987-88.

- Fred Pickering scored in a record 7 consecutive FA Cup games in 1964-65 and 1965-66.

FA Cup hat tricks for Everton

Only Graeme Sharp has scored a hat trick [in the 5-0 win at Sheffield Wednesday in 1987-88] in FA Cup ties played by Everton since the War. The full list is.

A Brady	v Derby County [h]	18 January 1890
Fred Geary	v Derby County [h]	18 January 1890
Alfred Milward	v Derby County [h]	18 January 1890
John Bell	v Southport [a]	2 February 1895
Jimmy Settle	v Southampton [h]	3 March 1905
H Bolton [4]	v Oldham Athletic [h]	5 February 1908
Tom Browell [4]	v Bury [h]	8 February 1912
Tom Browell	v Stockport County [h]	15 January 1913
Dixie Dean [4]	v Crystal Palace [a]	24 January 1931
Dixie Dean [4]	v Southport [h]	28 February 1931
Albert Geldard	v Grimsby Town [h]	12 January 1935
Jackie Coulter	v Sunderland [h]	30 January 1935
Tommy Lawton	v Doncaster Rovers [h]	21 January 1939
Graeme Sharp	v Sheffield Wednesday [h]	27 January 1988

FA Cup hat tricks against Everton

Of the 6 players who have scored FA Cup hat tricks against Everton, the most recent is Ian Storey-Moore, in a 3-2 defeat, in a classic Quarter Final tie at Nottingham Forest, in 1966-67.

Alf Edge	Stoke City [a]	1 February 1890
Marsh	Bolton Wanderers [a]	22 February 1908
Cook	Brighton [a]	2 February 1924
J Morrison	Tottenham Hotspur [a]	22 February 1937
Ron Wylie	Aston Villa [h]	14 February 1959
Ian Storey-Moore	Nottingham Forest [a]	8 April 1967

- In 1979-80, Bob Latchford set a new club record by scoring in every round of the FA Cup, up to, and including, the Semi Final. Strangely, for this most prolific of goalscorers, that season saw him score more FA and League Cup goals [7] than in the League [6].

- Pat Van Den Hauwe, against Blackburn, in the 1985-86 4th Round, was the last Everton player to score at both ends in an FA Cup tie, scoring his only Cup goal of his Everton career and putting through his own net as the Blues won 3-1.

Sent off

- In the 1979-80 campaign, Brian Kidd became the first player to be sent off twice in the FA Cup in the same season: against Wigan in the 4th Round and West Ham in the Semi Final.

- In the 3rd Round tie at Goodison, on 5 January 1997, Ian Culverhouse of Swindon was sent off after just 55 seconds, the quickest in FA Cup history.

- In the 1985 Final, Kevin Moran of Manchester United, was the first player to be sent off in an FA Cup Final at Wembley.

Most FA Cup appearances

Ten players have made 39 or more appearances for the club in the FA Cup.

Neville Southall	1981 – 1997	70 appearances
Kevin Ratcliffe	1980 – 1991	57 appearances
Jack Taylor	1896 – 1910	56 appearances
Graeme Sharp	1980 – 1991	54 appearances
Harry Makepeace	1903 – 1915	52 appearances
Dave Watson	1986 – 2000	48 appearances
Brian Labone	1957 – 1971	45 appearances
Jack Sharp	1899 – 1910	42 appearances
Gordon West	1962 – 1973	40 appearances
Alex Young	1901 – 1911	39 appearances

- The record for the most consecutive FA Cup ties played is by Jack Taylor, who made 48 consecutive appearances from 1896-97 – 1907-08. The post-War record is 36 consecutive games by Brian Labone [1963-64 – 1970-71] with Neville Southall [1986-87 – 1992-93] playing in 35 consecutive games.

- Brian Labone made a record 45 FA Cup appearances for the club without scoring a goal.

- Tommy Ring and Brian Borrows have both made a post-War record 27 League appearances, without appearing in a single FA Cup tie for the club.

EVERTON IN THE LEAGUE CUP

The League Cup

Everton have been relatively unsuccessful in this competition, having reached the Final on just 2 occasions since its inception in 1960, with one other losing Semi Final. The club did not compete in the tournament from 1961-62 – 1966-67 inclusive and also in 1970-71.

Everton's first opponents in the League Cup were Accrington Stanley, who had also been the Blues' first League opponents in 1888.

1977 Final v Aston Villa

- The 1977 Final against Aston Villa will go down in history as the only English domestic Final to go to a 2nd replay; Everton losing 3-2 at Old Trafford, after a 1-1 draw at Hillsborough and a goalless draw at Wembley.

- Bob Latchford's goals in both replays make him the only player to score in 2 replayed Finals in the 2 major Cup tournaments in this country.

- Roger Kenyon's own goal in the 1st replay was the first by any player in the Final. Brian Little was the 1st player to score twice in any domestic Final against Everton in the 2nd replay.

- Everton deployed a different right back in all 3 Final matches – Dave Jones [Wembley], Mike Bernard [Hillsborough] and Neil Robinson [Old Trafford].

- Dave Jones and Duncan McKenzie have the unfortunate distinction of playing for Everton in a Wembley Final and not picking up a medal of any sort, as neither player was involved in the deciding game at Old Trafford. Duncan McKenzie does not have happy memories of Wembley, as in his career, he was named as an England substitute on 13 occasions without winning a cap. He was also an unused substitute in Leeds United's 1975 European Cup Final, but did become the first Englishman to appear in a European Final for a foreign club, when appearing for Anderlecht in the 1976 Super Cup Final.

- Two Aston Villa players, John Gidman and Andy Gray, would later move to Everton. Gidman's 1985 FA Cup Final appearance for Manchester United against the Blues would make him the first [and, so far, only] player to appear against Everton for different sides in an FA Cup and League Cup Final.

1984 Final v Liverpool

- By drawing the first game 0-0 at Wembley, Everton and Liverpool made history by becoming the only clubs to have twice appeared in goalless draws at Wembley in the Final.

- Future FA Cup Final hero, Paul Rideout, had scored for Aston Villa in their 2nd leg game against the Blues at Villa Park. The Blues, however, won 2-1 on aggregate.

- Andy King's substitute appearance in the replay made him the only player to appear for Everton in both the 1977 and 1984 Finals.

Goalscoring

Everton's biggest win in the competition is the 8-0 win over Wimbledon in a 2nd Round match on 29 August 1978. This still remains Wimbledon's biggest defeat since they joined the League in 1977. Bob Latchford [5 goals] and Martin Dobson [3] were the Blues' goalscorers; it was the last occasion when 2 players scored hat tricks in the same match for Everton.

Hat trick scorers in the League Cup

Frank Wignall	v Tranmere Rovers [a]	21 December 1960
Bob Latchford [5]	v Wimbledon [h]	29 August 1978
Martin Dobson	v Wimbledon [h]	29 August 1978
Paul Wilkinson	v Newport County [a]	7 October 1986
Tony Cottee	v Wrexham [1st leg] [a]	25 September 1990
Graeme Sharp	v Wrexham [2nd leg] [h]	9 October 1990
Paul Rideout	v Lincoln City [a]	21 September 1993

● Alan Sunderland, in a 3rd Round replay for Arsenal, on 23 November 1982, is the only player to score a hat trick against Everton in the League Cup.

Leading goalscorers

Bob Latchford, with 19 goals in 28 matches, is the leading goalscorer for Everton in the League Cup. The following have scored 7 or more goals in the competition.

Bob Latchford	1974 – 1980	19 goals
Graeme Sharp	1981 – 1990	15 goals
Andy King	1976 – 1984	11 goals
Adrian Heath	1982 – 1988	11 goals
Tony Cottee	1988 – 1994	11 goals
Kevin Sheedy	1982 – 1991	9 goals
Martin Dobson	1974 – 1978	8 goals
Frank Wignall	1960 – 1961	7 goals
Paul Wilkinson	1986 – 1987	7 goals
Paul Rideout	1992 – 1995	7 goals
Dave Watson	1986 – 1998	7 goals

● The most goals in the League Cup in a single season for Everton is 7, shared by Frank Wignall in 1960-61 and Paul Wilkinson in 1986-87.

Scorers in both FA Cup and League Cup Semi Finals

Listed below are the 3 players who have scored in both Semi Finals for the Blues.

Duncan McKenzie v Bolton [League Cup 1976-77] and Liverpool [FA Cup 1976-77]

Bob Latchford v Bolton [League Cup 1976-77] and West Ham United [FA Cup 1979-80]

Adrian Heath v Southampton [FA Cup 1983-84] and Arsenal [League Cup 1987-88]

● Adrian Heath's goal in the 3-1 2nd Leg defeat at Highbury, in the 1987-88 Semi Final, means that he can uniquely claim to have scored in both FA Cup and League Cup Semi Finals on the same ground for Everton.

Heaviest defeats

The Blues' heaviest defeat in the League Cup is 4-1, which has happened on 3 occasions.

v Leeds United [a]   5th Round   18 January 1978
v Leeds United [h]   4th Round   4 December 1991
v Coventry City [a]   3rd Round   15 October 1997

Most appearances in the League Cup

Neville Southall has made a club record 65 appearances in the League Cup for Everton. Here are the top 10.

65	Neville Southall	1982 – 1997
48	Graeme Sharp	1981 – 1990
47	Kevin Ratcliffe	1980 – 1991
39	Dave Watson	1986 – 1998
35	Adrian Heath	1982 – 1988
34	Mike Lyons	1972 – 1981
32	Kevin Sheedy	1982 – 1991
30	Andy King	1976 – 1984
30	Gary Stevens	1981 – 1988
28	Bob Latchford	1974 – 1980

● Both Peter Reid and Kevin Richardson have appeared both for and against Everton in Semi Finals – Reid for Bolton Wanderers in 1977 and Richardson for Arsenal in 1988. They both appeared in the 1984 Semi Final against Aston Villa for the Blues.

Fixtures

- Arsenal and Aston Villa are Everton's most common opponents in the League Cup, having played both sides on 9 occasions, including replays. However, they have been drawn against Arsenal on 5 occasions, compared to 4 for the Villa.

- Arsenal have knocked Everton out of the competition on a record 3 occasions.

Met in the League Cup and FA Cup in the same season

Three teams have played against Everton in both the League Cup and FA Cup in the same season.

Middlesbrough	1977-78	Lost FA Cup tie,	Won League Cup tie
Newport County	1982-83	Won FA Cup tie,	Won League Cup tie
Wimbledon	1992-93	Lost FA Cup tie,	Won League Cup tie

EVERTON IN EUROPE

Everton in Europe

Everton have played in European competitions in 11 seasons, their only successful campaign being the glorious run in the 1984-85 Cup Winners' Cup.

European results

- On 9 of the 10 occasions when they have been knocked out of Europe they can claim to have been unlucky: 7 times by the odd goal over 2 legs and twice on the away goals rule.

- The only side to win by 2 goals on aggregate is Ujpest Dozsa [4-2], in the 1965-66 Fairs Cup. The 3-0 defeat in Hungary remains the Blues' heaviest defeat in European competition.

- Feyenoord are the only side Everton have been drawn against twice in European competition and they have beaten the Blues on aggregate on both occasions, with Everton failing to score in 4 matches.

- Feyenoord, in the 1979-80 UEFA Cup, 1st Round, became the only side to beat Everton in both the home and away legs of a European tie.

- Surprisingly, Everton are unbeaten in the 6 matches they have played against German sides in Europe, winning 2 and drawing 4 games.

- The 1970-71 European Cup 2nd Round tie, against Borussia Moenchengladbach, is the only European tie played by the Blues to go to penalties, Everton winning thanks to the heroics of goalkeeper Andy Rankin.

- Everton have faced just one English side, Manchester United, in the 1964-65 Fairs Cup, in European competition. They lost 3-2 on aggregate.

Summary of European results by opponents' country

	P	W	D	L	F	A
Austria	1	1	0	0	3	1
Czechoslovakia	4	3	0	1	6	2
Denmark	2	1	1	0	2	1
England	2	0	1	1	2	3
Germany	6	2	4	0	7	4
Greece	2	0	2	0	1	1
Holland	6	0	1	3	5	3
Hungary	2	1	0	1	2	4
Iceland	4	4	0	0	15	5
Ireland	4	4	0	0	11	0
Italy	4	0	2	2	0	2
Norway	2	2	0	0	9	4
Scotland	4	3	0	1	7	3
Spain	2	1	0	1	1	2
Totals	45	22	11	10	71	35

Biggest victories

Everton have scored 5 or more goals in a game on 4 occasions.

6-2	IB Keflavik [h]	16 September 1970	European Cup
5-0	Finn Harps [a]	12 September 1978	UEFA Cup
5-0	Finn Harps [h]	26 September 1978	UEFA Cup
5-2	Valerengens IF [a]	23 September 1964	Fairs Cup

Biggest defeats in European ties

0-3	Ujpest Dozsa [a]	November 3 1965	Fairs Cup
0-2	Dunfermline [a]	October 31 1962	Fairs Cup
0-2	Real Zaragoza [a]	November 9 1966	European Cup Winners' Cup

- The record aggregate defeat is 4-2 by Ujpest Dozsa in 1965-66.

1984-85 CUP WINNERS' CUP

- Everton were unbeaten in all 9 games they played in winning the competition. During this run they set a British record [which still stands] in Europe, of 7 matches without conceding a goal.

- In opening the scoring in the Final in Rotterdam, Andy Gray joined Peter Osgood [Chelsea] in the feat of scoring in both major domestic Cup Finals and a European Final. Future Everton player, Mark Hughes, would also later match this achievement.

- A substitute appearance at Goodison against Slovan Bratislava meant that Johnny Morrissey [Junior] joined Colin Harvey [Inter Milan 1963-64] in making his first team debut in a European game. Imre Varadi, in 1979-80 against Feyenoord, also achieved this.

- The classic line-up in the Final against Rapid Vienna had only played together on one other occasion in the competition: the 3-1 win against Bayern Munich in the Semi Final.

- The following players appeared for the Blues during the tournament, but did not feature in the Final: John Bailey, Terry Curran, Adrian Heath, Rob Wakenshaw, Alan Harper, Johnny Morrissey [Junior], Kevin Richardson and Ian Atkins.

- Andy Gray was the Blues' leading goalscorer in the tournament, with 5 goals.

Goalscoring

Two players have scored hat tricks for Everton in European competition.

Alan Ball	v IB Keflavik [h]	16 September 1970	European Cup
Andy Gray	v Fortuna Sittard [h]	6 March 1985	Euopean Cup Winners' Cup

- The Blues' leading scorer in European competition is Fred Pickering, with 6 goals, all in the Fairs' Cup competition of 1964-65. The leading scorer in one tie, is Joe Royle, with 4 goals in the 2 legs against IB Keflavik, in 1970-71.

- Johnny Morrissey is the only player to have scored for Everton in each of the 3 major European competitions.

- Micky Walsh, signed from Blackpool in 1978, scored more goals for Everton in Europe than he did in domestic matches. His 2 goals against Finn Harps, in the UEFA Cup in 1978-79, eclipsing his only League goal scored against Aston Villa in the same season.

- The youngest goalscorer in European competition is David Johnson, who was 19 years 138 days old when scoring against Panathaniakos on 9 March 1971.

Leading scorers in European competition

Fred Pickering	6 goals	1964 – 1965
Andy Gray	5 goals	1984 – 1985
Alan Ball	4 goals	1966 – 1971
Joe Royle	4 goals	1970 – 1971
Andy King	4 goals	1978 – 1979
Graeme Sharp	4 goals	1984 – 1985
Johnny Morrissey	3 goals	1962 – 1971
Alex Young	3 goals	1962 – 1966
Bob Latchford	3 goals	1975 – 1979

Most appearances in Europe

Colin Harvey	19 appearances	1963 – 1971
Brian Labone	19 appearances	1962 – 1971
Johnny Morrissey	17 appearances	1962 – 1971
Tommy Wright	17 appearances	1964 – 1971
Derek Temple	16 appearances	1963 – 1966
Jimmy Gabriel	15 appearances	1962 – 1966
Neville Southall	13 appearances	1984 – 1995
Gordon West	13 appearances	1962 – 1970
Alex Young	13 appearances	1962 – 1966

- Gordon West, Colin Harvey and Brian Labone were the only players to appear for the Blues in both their European Cup campaigns of 1963-64 and 1970-71.

- The youngest player to appear for Everton in Europe is Rob Wakenshaw, who was 18 years 283 days when he came on as substitute against UC Dublin on 2 October 1984.

- Although in their time together at the club Gordon West [386 domestic games] was the usual number one goalkeeping choice, ahead of Andy Rankin [92], in Europe he made just one more appearance: 13 against the 12 of Rankin.

- When Andy Rankin came on for Gordon West against Nuremburg, on 12 October 1965, it was the first case of a goalkeeping substitute in the club's history, the next instance would be over 27 years later, at Queens Park Rangers, in December 1992 [see Appearances chapter].

- Neville Southall was the only player to appear for the club in European competition, both before and after the ban on English clubs from 1985 to 1990.

- Three Everton players have appeared in a European Cup Final for a different club: Brian Kidd [Manchester United, 1968], David Johnson [Liverpool, 1981] and Ken McNaught [Aston Villa, 1982]. Duncan McKenzie was an unused substitute for Leeds United in 1975.

- In the 1995-96 season, Regi Blinker appeared against Everton in both the Premiership and Europe, playing for Feyenoord in the Cup Winners' Cup and Sheffield Wednesday in the Premiership.

Sent off in Europe

Three players have been sent off in European matches involving the Blues.

Preben Larson	for AaB Aalborg	European Cup Winners' Cup 1966
Johnny Morrissey	v Real Zaragoza	European Cup Winners' Cup 1966
Mike Bernard	v AC Milan	UEFA Cup 1975

EVERTON IN OTHER COMPETITIONS

CHARITY SHIELD

Everton have appeared in the Charity Shield on 11 occasions, winning the trophy 8 times, losing twice and sharing it once.

1928	Won 2-1	Blackburn Rovers
1932	Won 5-3	Newcastle United
1933	Lost 0-3	Arsenal
1963	Won 4-0	Manchester United
1966	Lost 0-1	Liverpool
1970	Won 2-1	Chelsea
1984	Won 1-0	Liverpool
1985	Won 2-0	Manchester United
1986	Drew 1-1	Liverpool
1987	Won 1-0	Coventry City
1995	Won 1-0	Blackburn Rovers

Appearances
- Everton were the first club to appear in 4 consecutive Charity Shields at Wembley, following the move to the stadium in 1974.
- Kevin Ratcliffe, Trevor Steven, Graeme Sharp and Adrian Heath have all appeared in 4 Charity Shields [all 1984 – 1987].
- Gerry Glover's appearance in the 1966 game was one of only 4 first-team appearances for the club.
- The first occurrence of an Everton substitute being substituted, was in the 1986 game, when Neil Adams, on for Kevin Sheedy, was replaced by Paul Wilkinson.

Goals
- Dixie Dean scored a record 4 goals in the 1932 match.
- Adrian Heath, in 1985 and 1986, is the only player to score in 2 games at Wembley.
- Everton's winner in the 1984 game is officially credited as a Bruce Grobbelaar own-goal.

Results
- After defeating Manchester United 4-0 in the 1963 game, the Blues lost 5-1 at Old Trafford, in a League match, a fortnight later.
- Everton's only 2 defeats have come at Goodison Park.

TEXACO CUP

Everton made their only appearance in this Anglo-Scottish tournament when losing 1-0 on aggregate to Hearts in 1973-74.

SCREEN-SPORT SUPER CUP

This competition was organised to compensate those clubs who had missed out on a place in Europe following the ban on English clubs in 1985. Although scheduled for the 1985-86 season, the competition drifted into the following campaign, when the Blues met Liverpool in the Final.

- The Blues lost 7-2 on aggregate to Liverpool in the Final, although Kevin Sheedy set a record of sorts by becoming the only Everton player to score in 2 post-War matches, at Anfield, in the same season. He scored in the 1st leg of the Final in September 1986, and in the League game the following April. Both goals were free kicks, and both in front of the Kop.

- Trevor Steven missed a penalty in the 2nd leg of the Final at Goodison, although a 2nd penalty was scored by Graeme Sharp.

- Darren Coyle played in both Semi Final games against Tottenham, even though he never played in a League or Cup game for the Blues.

FULL MEMBERS CUP

The Blues made their only appearance in this competition in 1986-87, losing on penalties to Charlton Athletic at Goodison in Round 2. The opening round had been notable for a first-half hat trick for Graeme Sharp, against Newcastle.

SIMOD CUP

- Everton competed twice in this competition and in 1989 reached the Final against Nottingham Forest at Wembley, losing 4-3, with Tony Cottee scoring twice.

- The home match against Millwall, on 20 December 1988, saw a post-War record Goodison low crowd of 3,703 and a goalkeeping appearance by Mike Stowell, who never played a League or Cup match for the club.

ZENITH DATA SYSTEMS CUP

- The Blues reached the Final of this competition in 1990-91 where they lost 4-1 to Crystal Palace at Wembey, with Robert Warzycha scoring.

- The Quarter Final game against Sunderland was won 4-0, with Tony Cottee scoring all 4 goals.

FA YOUTH CUP

Everton have appeared in the final of this competition on 6 occasions.

1960-61	Lost 3-5	Chelsea
1964-65	Won 3-2	Arsenal
1976-77	Lost 0-1	Crystal Palace
1982-83	Lost 0-1	Norwich City [replay after 5-5 agg]
1983-84	Won 4-2	Stoke City
1997-98	Won 5-3	Blackburn Rovers

[scores given are aggregate results]

- In the 1961 Final Everton lost to a Chelsea side featuring both Terry Venables and Ron 'Chopper' Harris.

- The victorious 1965 side included future title-winners, John Hurst and Jimmy Husband, the latter having made his first team debut 9 days before the Final. Geoff Barnett, who was the Blues' keeper, would later play for the Gunners in the 1972 FA Cup Final. John Radford was a scorer for Arsenal.

- The losing 1977 team included future club captain, Mark Higgins, as well as Joe McBride. The only goal of the Final was scored by future England international, Terry Fenwick.

- The stars of the 1997-98 line-up included Francis Jeffers, Danny Cadamarteri and Richard Dunne.

Common opponents

- Between 30 October 1984 and 18 September 1985, Everton played Manchester United in 5 different competitions – the League Cup, League, FA Cup, Charity Shield and the Screen Sport Super Cup.

- United are the only side that Everton have met in 6 tournaments – the above 5, plus the Inter Cities Fairs Cup.

- In the 1986-87 season, Everton played Liverpool on no less than 6 occasions – twice in the League, twice in the Screen Sport Super Cup, the Charity Shield and the League Cup.

FIXTURES

Everton's 10 most common opponents in League matches

Aston Villa	172 games
Liverpool	164 games
Arsenal	160 games
Manchester United	144 games
Manchester City	138 games
Sunderland	138 games
Newcastle United	134 games
West Bromwich Albion	132 games
Sheffield Wednesday	128 games
Tottenham Hotspur	128 games

- Everton against Aston Villa is the most commonly played League fixture in English football.

- Everton have faced the following clubs in just one season of League football: Bristol Rovers [1953-54], Carlisle United [1974-75], Glossop [1899-1900], Leyton Orient [1962-63], Northampton Town [1965-66], Port Vale [1930-31] and Reading [1930-31].

- The last occasion when Everton met a side for the first time in a League match, was against Wimbledon, on 13 September 1986, in a 2-1 win at Plough Lane.

- The biggest gap between League fixtures with a club was 68 years between playing Bradford City in 1930-31 and 1999-00.

- The record for consecutive home fixtures in the League is 6, between 3 January 1903 and 14 March 1903. During this period, 2 FA Cup matches were played at Goodison, taking the run to 8 consecutive home matches in all competitions.

- The club played 5 consecutive away matches in the League from 13 January 1894 to 3 March 1894. One FA Cup match was played at Stoke during this period, taking the run to 6 matches away from home.

Fixture congestion

● The record for the most competitive fixtures in a season is 62, in the 1984-85 season [42 League, 7 FA Cup, 4 League Cup, 9 Cup Winners' Cup].

● The Blues have twice played 9 League fixtures in a month: in April 1963 [P9, W5, D4] and April 1969 [P9, W4, D4, L1].

● The last time as many as 9 fixtures were played in a calendar month was in January 1988, when the Blues played 3 League games, 5 FA Cup games and 1 League Cup match.

● The greatest number of games played against the same side in a calendar month is 5 [1 League, 4 FA Cup] against Sheffield Wednesday in January 1988.

● The longest gap between scheduled League fixtures is 63 days, between playing Preston at home on 10 January 1891 and the final match of the season, at Burnley, on 14 March.

● The longest gap in the post-War period between League fixtures is 51 days, between 22 December 1962 and 12 February 1963, due to poor weather. January 1963 is the only month, during the club's post-War history, when no League fixture was played – although 2 FA Cup matches were played.

Repeat fixtures

● The last occasion Everton played the same side in consecutive League fixtures, in the same season, was against Norwich City on 19 April and 30 April 1977.

Abandoned games

Arsenal 1 Everton 3	26 November 1904	75 mins
Everton 1 Stockport 1 [FA Cup]	11 January 1913	48 mins [snow]
Tottenham Hotspur 1 Everton 1	17 December 1969	30 mins [floodlights]
Bolton Wanderers 1 Everton 1	1 January 1979	45 mins [pitch]

● The abandoned game against Spurs was itself the 2nd attempt at the fixture, the original being postponed on 29 November 1969.

● The game against Arsenal was one of the most controversial in the club's history, for when it was replayed, on 22 April 1905, Everton lost 2-1 and would lose the title by a point from Newcastle.

● For the record, the results when the other games were finally replayed were: Stockport [Won 5-1], Tottenham Hotspur [Won 1-0] and Bolton Wanderers [Lost 1-3].

Christmas Day games

- Everton's last fixture on Christmas Day was a 1-1 draw against Bolton Wanderers, in 1957.

- The biggest victory on Christmas Day was 7-0 against Derby, in 1936. The biggest defeat was a 0-6 loss at White Hart Lane, in 1956.

Boxing Day games

- Some of the club's biggest defeats have occurred on Boxing Day: 3-7 against Newcastle in 1933 and 0-7 against Sunderland 12 months later. The Blues were also beaten 6-2 at Birmingham in 1955.

- Between 1987 and 1995, Everton played away from home on this date on just one occasion – a 1-0 win at Derby – compared to 7 games at home.

New Years Day games

- The 2-1 win at Chelsea, in 1991, was the first away win on New Years day in 18 away games since 1897.

Easter games

- Everton last played home games on consecutive days when they drew 1-1 with West Bromwich Albion, on 27 March 1964, and beat Blackpool 3-1 on Good Friday, 24 hours later.

- Everton are unbeaten in the 7 matches played on a Good Friday against Liverpool – winning 2 and drawing 5.

- The last occasion when Everton played 3 fixtures over Easter, was 24 – 27 March 1978, when the 3 games against Newcastle, Leeds and Manchester United were all won. This was the last instance of the Blues playing 3 fixtures in 4 days.

Opening day fixtures

- Everton's biggest victory on the opening day of the season, was 5-0 against Manchester United, on 27 August 1921. The biggest defeat was 5-1 at Leeds, on 18 August 1956.

- The Blues failed to win at home on the opening day from 1967 to 1981.

- The 2-0 win at Southampton on the opening day of the 1993-94 season was the first win away from home since 1978.

- Between 1960 and 1972 the fixture list certainly favoured pairing Everton and Manchester United together at the beginning of the season: 1960-61 [twice in the opening 4 games], 1962-63 [twice in the opening 4 games], 1963-64 [2nd game], 1964-65 [twice in the opening 8 games], 1966-67 [twice in the opening 4 games], 1967-68 [opening game], 1968-69 [opening game], 1969-70 [twice in the opening 4 games], 1970-71 and 1971-72 [6th game], 1972-73 [3rd game].

- The earliest opening day of the season was 8 August 1999, when Everton drew 1-1 with Manchester United at Goodison.

Wembley games

The club's full record at Wembley, including ZDS and Simod Cup matches.

	P	W	D	L	F	A
FA Cup	8	4	0	4	12	10
League Cup	2	0	2	0	0	0
Charity Shield	5	4	1	0	6	1
Simod Cup	1	0	0	1	3	4
ZDS Cup	1	0	0	1	1	4
Totals	17	8	3	6	22	19

- Liverpool have been the Blues' most common opponents at Wembley, playing them on 5 occasions [2 FA Cup, 1 League Cup, 2 Charity Shield]. Manchester United [2 FA Cup, 1 Charity Shield] are next.

- Kevin Ratcliffe has made the most appearances with 11 [4 FA Cup, 1 League Cup, 4 Charity Shield, 1 Simod, 1 ZDS].

THE DERBY

EVERTON V LIVERPOOL LEAGUE RECORD

One of the oldest competitive fixtures in English football, the sides had met 164 times in the League at the end of the 2000-01 season. The first League derby was played in October 1894 and was watched by 44,000 spectators. The Blues won 3-0.

Head to head

Home	Everton	Won 31	Drew 27	Lost 24
Away	Everton	Won 23	Drew 24	Lost 35

Home

The defeat by Liverpool in 2001 was the first since 1990. The previous 9 League meetings had seen 4 Everton wins and 5 draws.

Away

Everton have won only twice since 1986 – in November 1995 and September 1999 – although the Blues have chalked up more wins at Anfield than any other away side.

Everton

Goals

Dixie Dean	18
Alex Young [1901 – 1911]	9
Jimmy Settle	8
Bobby Parker	6
Jack Taylor	5
Duncan Ferguson	4
Graeme Sharp	4
Tommy Lawton	4
Roy Vernon	4

Hat tricks

Alex Young [4] [h]	1 April 1904
Bobby Parker [a]	3 October 1914
Dixie Dean [a]	25 February 1928
Dixie Dean [a]	19 September 1931

Liverpool

Goals

Ian Rush	13
Harry Chambers	8
Dick Forshaw	7
Jack Balmer	6

Hat tricks

Harry Chambers [a]	7 October 1922
Dick Forshaw [a]	26 September 1925
Harold Barton [a]	11 February 1933
Fred Howe [4] [a]	7 September 1935
Ian Rush [4] [h]	6 November 1982

Everton goals

- Andrei Kanchelskis was the last Everton player to score in both League derbies in a season, doing so in 1995-96. His 2 goals at Anfield, on his derby debut, can be added to his achievements of scoring the last hat trick in a Manchester derby and also being the only player to score in a Merseyside, Manchester and Glasgow derby.

- The last Everton player to score in 3 consecutive League derbies was Andy King, in both games in 1978-79, and the first derby of the following season.

- The last Everton player to score in consecutive League derby matches at Goodison is Maurice Johnstone, in the 1-1 draw on 28 December 1991, and the 2-1 win 12 months later.

- The last Everton player to score in consecutive derby matches at Anfield is Kevin Campbell, in 1999-00 and 2000-01.

- The last Everton player to score twice at Goodison in a League derby is Alan Ball, on 27 August 1966.

- Gary Lineker scored in all 3 of the derby matches he played for Everton. In the 1985-86 season he scored in both League games and the FA Cup Final.

- Prior to Gary Lineker, the only player to score for Everton in League and FA Cup derby matches, in the same season, was Walter Abbott in the 1905-06 campaign.

- David Johnson and Peter Beardsley are the only 2 players who have scored for both sides in derby games.

- The 2-1 win at Goodison, on 7 December 1992, with Peter Beardsley scoring the winner, is the only post-War derby in which Everton have come from behind to win.

- Everton's youngest derby match scorer is Tommy Lawton, who was 17 years 362 days old when he scored at Anfield, on 2 October 1937.

- The youngest scorer in the post-War era is Francis Jeffers, who was 18 years 68 days old when he scored at Anfield, on 3 April 1999.

- The most unproductive spell in League derby matches was the 13 games without a victory following David Johnson's winner for the Blues at Goodison, on 13 November 1971, which was finally ended by Andy King, at home, on 28 October 1978.

- In the 13-game sequence without a League derby victory, from 1971 to 1978, the only Everton player who scored against Liverpool was Martin Dobson, in a 3-1 loss at Anfield on 16 October 1976.

- Mick Lyons played in 18 League and 2 FA Cup derby games, from 1972-82, without being on a winning side.

Everton's biggest League victories in the derby

5-0 [h]   9 April 1909
5-0 [a]   3 October 1913

● The last time Everton scored 4 times in the fixture in the League was a 4-0 win at Anfield, on 19 September 1964.

● No less than 69 League derbies, up to the end of the 2000-01 campaign, had been played since Everton last scored 3 times, in a 3-1 victory at Goodison, on 27 August 1966.

Biggest League defeats in the derby
● The Blues' biggest defeat was a 6-0 loss at Anfield, on 7 September 1935.

● The heaviest defeat at Goodison was the infamous 5-0 loss on 6 November 1982.

● The 7-4 loss at Anfield, on 11 February 1933, provided a record number of goals [11] for a single fixture in the series.

Sequences of results
● The Blues longest streak of unbeaten League derby matches was the 14 in the 7 seasons from 1899-00 to 1906-07 inclusive.

● Everton were unbeaten in a remarkable 15 League derbies at Anfield, between the 1899-00 and 1914-15 seasons, winning 10 and drawing 5 matches.

● In recent years, the longest unbeaten streak is 9 League derbies unbeaten from 1994.

● The last League 'double' over Liverpool was in 1984-85, with 1-0 victories at both Goodison and Anfield.

● The last time Everton lost both League derbies in a season was in 2000-01.

Weekday derbies

The Blues' 3-2 loss at Goodison, on Easter Monday 2001, brought to an end an extraordinary run of 12 League derbies unbeaten on weekdays.

Tuesday 13 March 1979	Drew 1-1 [a]
Thursday 23 May 1985	Won 1-0 [h]
Wednesday 3 May 1989	Drew 0-0 [h]
Monday 7 December 1992	Won 2-1 [h]
Tuesday 21 November 1995	Drew 2-0 [h]
Tuesday 24 January 1995	Drew 0-0 [h]
Tuesday 16 April 1996	Drew 1-1 [h]
Wednesday 20 November 1996	Drew 1-1 [a]
Wednesday 16 April 1997	Drew 1-1 [h]
Monday 23 February 1998	Drew 1-1 [a]
Monday 27 September 1999	Won 1-0 [a]
Friday 21 April 2000	Drew 0-0 [h]

Own goals conceded by Everton in League derby games

Sandy Brown [h]	6 December 1969
Tommy Wright [a]	4 March 1972
John McLaughlin [a]	4 March 1972
Mike Lyons [a]	20 October 1979
John Bailey [a]	21 March 1981
Claus Thomsen [h]	12 April 1997

- Merseyside fans had to wait until the spectacular diving header of Sandy Brown, in December 1969, to witness the first own goal in a League derby. He remains the only player to have scored at both the correct and wrong end of the pitch in derby games.

- The only own goal in derby games, prior to that, had been Walter Balmer, in the FA Cup tie at Goodison, on 8 February 1905.

- Neil Ruddock, at Goodison on 18 October 1997, is the only player to concede an own goal for Liverpool in a League derby, although Bruce Grobbelaar is credited with scoring one in the 1984 Charity Shield.

Penalties

Only 3 Everton players have scored from the spot in post-War League derby games.

Roy Vernon [h]	22 September 1962
Wayne Clarke [a]	11 December 1988
David Unsworth [h]	16 April 2001

- The last Everton player to miss was Graeme Sharp, whose kick was saved by Bruce Grobbelaar at Goodison, on 3 March 1984.

- Liverpool have scored 12 League penalties in derby games.

Most derbies

Players who have appeared in the most League derbies for Everton.

Neville Southall	31
Dave Watson	24
Jack Taylor	24
Ted Sagar	19
Kevin Ratcliffe	18
Jack Sharp	18
Harry Makepeace	18
Mike Lyons	18
Gordon West	18

Debutants

Surely one of the most daunting experiences in the career of a player is his debut, especially so if it is made in a League derby. Everton have 17 players who have made either their League debut, or their first appearance for the club, in a derby match.

Bob Menham*	21 November 1896
R Turner	9 April 1909
J Allan	12 February 1910
Walter Scott	12 February 1910
J Houston*	8 February 1913
G Harrison	20 September 1913
Bobby Irvine*	12 November 1921
Jerry Kelly*	12 February 1927
Edward Taylor	12 February 1927
E Common*	9 February 1929
Lachie McPherson	4 January 1930
William Higgins	21 September 1946
Bernie Wright	4 March 1972
Glenn Keeley	6 November 1982
Ibrahim Bakayoko*	17 October 1998
Kevin Campbell	3 April 1999
Scot Gemmill	3 April 1999

[* indicates League debut in England]

● Turner celebrated with a goal.

● Glenn Keeley was sent off 37 minutes into his only appearance in a blue shirt, in what was one of the briefest careers in Everton history.

● Paul Bracewell made his first appearance for Everton against Liverpool at Wembley in the 1984 Charity Shield and his last in the 1989 FA Cup Final against the same club.

● Neil Adams, Kevin Langley and Paul Power all made their Everton debuts in the 1986 Charity Shield against Liverpool.

Played for both sides

Eleven players have appeared in the derby for both sides, Nick Barmby being the most recent to achieve this feat.

	Everton derby debut	Liverpool career
Edgar Chadwick	17 November 1894	1902 – 1904
Bill Lacey	27 December 1910	1912 – 1924
Dick Forshaw	15 October 1927	1919 – 1927
Tom Johnson	19 September 1931	1934 – 1936
David Johnson	13 November 1971	1977 – 1982
Steve McMahon	18 October 1980	1985 – 1991
Peter Beardsley	31 August 1991	1987 – 1991
Gary Ablett	7 December 1992	1987 – 1991
David Burrows	24 January 1995	1988 – 1993
Don Hutchsion	17 October 1998	1992 – 1994
Nick Barmby	20 November 1996	2000 –

Sent off in League derbies

Terry McDermott [a]	20 October 1979	Liverpool
Gary Stanley [a]	20 October 1979	Everton
Eamonn O'Keefe [a]	7 November 1981	Everton
Glenn Keeley [h]	6 November 1982	Everton
David Unsworth [h]	12 April 1997	Everton
Robbie Fowler [h]	12 April 1997	Liverpool
Sander Westerveld [a]	27 September 1999	Liverpool
Francis Jeffers [a]	27 September 1999	Everton
Steven Gerrard [a]	27 September 1999	Liverpool
Thomas Gravesen [a]	29 October 2000	Everton
Igor Biscan [h]	16 April 2001	Liverpool

● Despite the fiery nature of the occasion, it was not until 1979 that a player was sent off in the fixture. On that occasion it was 2 players, Gary Stanley of Everton, and Terry McDermott of Liverpool, who were sent off in a 20-man brawl, on 20 October 1979, in a game that also featured a memorable Mike Lyons' own goal and a streaker.

● Robbie Fowler and David Unsworth were sent off for fighting at Goodison on 12 April 1997.

● At Anfield, on 27 September 1999, both Sander Westerveld and Francis Jeffers were given the marching orders for brawling, and later in the same game, Steven Gerrard was also shown the red card.

FA CUP DERBY GAMES

The clubs have been drawn together on an FA Cup record, 15 occasions, and the 20 games [including replays] in the competition is also a record. The neutral club grounds in the list below, relate to FA Cup Semi Finals.

	P	W	D	L	F	A
Goodison	10	5	1	4	13	16
Anfield	3	0	3	0	3	3
Villa Park	1	1	0	0	2	0
Maine Road	3	0	1	2	2	7
Old Trafford	1	0	0	1	1	2
Wembley	2	0	0	2	3	6
Total	20	6	5	9	24	34

- There have been no hat tricks or sendings-off between the 2 sides in FA Cup games. No Everton player has scored a penalty in the post-War era.

A brace in the FA Cup derby

Players who have scored twice in Everton matches against Liverpool in the FA Cup.

Alex Young [h]	4 February 1911	2nd Round
Stuart McCall [Wembley]	20 May 1989	Final
Graeme Sharp [h]	27 February 1991	5th Round
Tony Cottee [h]	27 February 1991	5th Round

- Harold Hardman [1904-05 and 1905-06] and Alan Ball [1966-67 and 1970-71] are the only players to score against Liverpool for the Blues in 2 different FA Cup ties.

- Two players, Kevin Ratcliffe and Graeme Sharp, have appeared in a club record, 6 FA Cup derby games.

LEAGUE CUP DERBY GAMES

Surprisingly, the clubs have been drawn together only 3 times in the League Cup, with one being the 1984 final at Wembley.

Wembley	0-0	Final	25 March 1984
Maine Road	0-1	Replay	29 March 1984
Goodison	0-1	5th Round	21 January 1987
Anfield	1-0	3rd Round	28 October 1987

- Gary Stevens, at Anfield, in 1987, is the only Everton player to score against Liverpool in the competition.

Attendances

- The record crowd for a League derby game – and the highest crowd ever at Goodison – is 78,299 for the game on 18 September 1948. However, as noted in the FA Cup section, over 100,000 people saw the 1967 home FA Cup tie with the help of a closed-circuit link-up at Anfield.

- The highest crowds for a derby game anywhere have been at Wembley, with 100,000 witnessing the 1984 League Cup Final and Charity Shield.

Derby match summary

The following provides a summary of most goals and appearances for Everton in derby games in the League, FA Cup, League Cup and Charity Shield.

Goals

Dixie Dean	19	Graeme Sharp	6
Alex Young [1901 – 1911]	12	Alan Ball	5
Jimmy Settle	8	Jack Taylor	5
Bobby Parker	6		

- Graeme Sharp also scored a goal in the 1986-87 Screen-Sport Super Cup Final.

Appearances

Neville Southall	41
Kevin Ratcliffe	30
Dave Watson	30
Jack Taylor	29
Graeme Sharp	28
Jack Sharp	23
Harry Makepeace	22
Alex Young [1901 – 1911]	22
Cohn Harvey	20
Mike Lyons	20
Ted Sagar	20
Kevin Sheedy	20
Gordon West	20

- Kevin Ratcliffe, Graeme Sharp and Kevin Sheedy also played in 2 Screen-Sport Super Cup games against Liverpool in 1986-87.

- Steven McMahon played in 18 games for Liverpool [plus 2 Screen-Sport Super Cup matches] and 7 games for Everton.

Other achievements

- Despite many publications stating that Steve McMahon was the first player to captain both Everton and Liverpool [although he failed to do so in a derby game], in the early days of the League, Andrew Hannah captained both clubs, although again, not in the derby.

- In March 1988, a goal from Wayne Clarke at Goodison meant that Liverpool only equalled Leeds United's record of 29 games unbeaten from the start of the season, set in 1973-74. That Leeds team featured Allan Clarke, the older brother of Wayne.

- Richard Gough has played in derby games in Dundee [for United], London [for Spurs], Glasgow [for Rangers] and Merseyside [for Everton].

- Joe Royle never lost a derby match as Everton manager, winning 2 and drawing 3 of his 5 games.

- When Paul Gerrard [Everton] and Steven Gerrard [Liverpool] were in opposition at Anfield on 27 September 1999, it was the first instance of opposing players having the same surname in the match since Ernie Hunt [Everton] and Roger Hunt [Liverpool] played in the derby of 3 February 1968.

- The April 1976 clash had an 11am kick-off, due to the Grand National at Aintree that afternoon.

- The first Everton substitute to be deployed in a derby was Gerry Glover, who replaced Brian Labone in September 1965.

- Sandy Brown holds 2 derby 'firsts' – the first own goal in a League derby and, on 27 August 1966, he was the first substitute to score in the fixture, in a 3-1 win for Everton.

EVERTON RESULTS

Biggest victories in all competitions

11-2	Derby County [h] [FA Cup]	8 January 1890
9-1	Manchester City [h]	3 September 1906
9-1	Plymouth Argyle [h]	27 December 1930
9-1	Southport [h] [FA Cup]	28 February 1931
9-2	Leicester City [h]	28 November 1931
9-3	Sheffield Wednesday [h]	17 October 1931
8-0	Stoke City [h]	2 November 1889
8-0	Southampton [h]	20 November 1971
8-0	Wimbledon [h] [League Cup]	29 August 1978
8-0	Doncaster Rovers [h] [FA Cup]	21 January 1939
8-1	Darwen [h]	21 October 1893
8-1	Sheffield Wednesday [h]	23 December 1893
8-1	Newcastle United [h]	31 October 1931
8-3	Cardiff City [h]	28 April 1962
8-4	Plymouth Argyle [h]	27 February 1954

- In 1890 Everton played Derby County on 4 occasions, winning all 4 games and scoring 27 goals in the process – 11-2, 3-0, 7-0 and 6-2.

- In the 9-1 win against Southport, in 1930, the Blues led 7-0 at half-time.

- The last occasion Everton scored 7 times in a match was the 7-1 victory over Southampton, in a League match, on 16 November 1996.

- The last time Everton scored 6 times in a game was the 6-0 home win over West Ham, on 8 May 1999.

The Blues' biggest victories away from home

7-0	Charlton Athletic	7 February 1931
6-0	Crystal Palace [FA Cup]	4 January 1931
6-1	Derby County	5 November 1892
6-2	Derby County	13 December 1890
6-2	Derby County	13 February 1954
6-2	West Bromwich Albion	16 March 1968

- The above wins against Derby County are the only instances of a side scoring 6 or more goals in 3 different away games against the same club.

Biggest defeats in all competitions

4-10	Tottenham Hotspur [a]	11 October 1958
2-8	Huddersfield Town [a]	7 April 1953
2-8	Newcastle United [a]	7 November 1959
0-7	Sunderland [a]	26 December 1934
0-7	Wolverhampton Wanderers [a]	22 February 1939
0-7	Portsmouth [a]	10 September 1949
2-7	Wolverhampton Wanderers [a]	13 February 1937
3-7	Derby County [a]	9 September 1893
3-7	Sunderland [a]	10 October 1925
3-7	Newcastle United [a]	5 March 1927
3-7	Newcastle United [h]	26 December 1933

● In the 8-2 defeat by Huddersfield, Jimmy Glazzard scored 4 headed goals for the opposition, one of the few instances in League history. He would sign for Everton 3 years later, but made only 3 League appearances for the club.

● The 10-4 game against Tottenham remains the highest number of goals scored in a top-flight match in the post-War era.

● The last time Everton conceded 6 goals in a League match was against Aston Villa, in a 2-6 loss, on 5 November 1989.

The Blues' biggest home defeats

3-7	Newcastle United	26 December 1933
0-6	Newcastle United	26 October 1912
0-6	Crystal Palace [FA Cup]	7 January 1922
1-6	Arsenal	6 September 1958
2-6	Manchester City	15 September 1928
2-6	Manchester United	26 December 1977

● The last occasion Everton conceded 5 goals in a home game was in the 5-1 defeat by Norwich City, on 25 September 1993.

High scoring draws
Everton have been involved in 2 of the 14 top-flight matches to have been drawn 5-5.

5-5	Derby County	15 October 1898
5-5	Sheffield Wednesday	12 November 1904

Most League victories in a season

Unless otherwise stated, the records for most defeats, victories and draws in a season relate to those seasons that had at least 38 games.

- Everton won 29 League matches in 1969-70, a club record. Eight games were drawn and only 5 lost.
- Eighteen home League wins in a season were achieved in 1930-31, 1931-32 and 1967-68.
- The most away League victories in a season is 12, recorded in both 1969-70 and 1984-85.
- In 1984-85 Everton set a new English club record by recording 43 victories in a season: 28 League, 5 FA Cup, 2 League Cup, 7 in the European Cup Winners' Cup, plus a Charity Shield game. This record still stands today. Even Manchester United, in their treble triumph of 1998-99, recorded only 36 victories.

Fewest League victories in a season

- The least number of victories in a full League season is 9 in 1971-72 [42 games]. Nine victories were also achieved in 1997-98, when the season was 38 matches.
- Just 5 home matches were won in the 1957-58 season, which broke the record set in 1929-30.
- Everton played out the 1959-60 season without recording a single victory away from home [8 draws and 13 defeats]. Only one away victory has been recorded on 5 occasions, the last being in 1971-72.

Most League defeats

- The greatest number of League defeats in a season is 22 in 1950-51, when the Blues were relegated, and also in 1993-94.
- The highest number of home defeats in a season is 9 out of 19 games in 1912-13, and 9 out of 21 home matches in 1947-48, 1950-51 and 1993-94.
- The record for away defeats in a season is 17 in 1936-37.

Fewest League defeats

- The fewest League defeats in a season is 5 in 1969-70 [1 at home, 4 away].
- The fewest home defeats in a season is in 1962-63, when Everton were unbeaten at home for the only time.
- The fewest away defeats in a season is 4, which was achieved in 1953-54 [Division 2], 1968-69 and 1969-70.

Draws

- The most drawn matches in a season is 18, set in 1925-26 and equalled in 1971-72 and 1974-75.

- The greatest number of 0-0 draws in a League season is 9, set in 1971-72. Eight out of the first 21 League matches were goalless in 1998-99, but at least one goal was scored in the last 17 games of the season.

- The least number of drawn games in a season is 4, set in 1928-29 and equalled in 1931-32 and 1958-59.

Winning sequences

- The club record for consecutive victories in League matches is 12 from 24 March 1894 to 13 October 1894 and post-War, 10 from 23 March 198 5to 8 May 1985.

- The record is 13, set by Spurs in 1960.

- The best start to a League season is 8 consecutive victories in the 1894-95 season. The best start to a post-War season is just 4 victories, in 1962-63 and 1969-70.

Home victories

- 15 consecutive home League victories were achieved in Division 2, from 4 October 1930, to 4 April 1931. The Blues also won 2 FA Cup matches in this period, taking the run to 17 consecutive victories.

- The post-War record – and the most in the top-flight – is 14 consecutive home League wins from 18 November 1967, to the first game of the following season, on 13 August 1968. The Blues also won an FA Cup game in this period, taking the run to 15 consecutive home wins.

Away victories

- The longest run of away League victories is 6, achieved in 1908-09 and in the last 4 matches of the 1914-15 season and the first 2 of the 1919-20 season, when football resumed after World War 1.

- The post-War record is 5 consecutive League away wins between 7 March 1970 and 4 April 1970.

Unbeaten sequences

- The longest unbeaten League run in the club's history is 20 matches between 29 April and 16 December 1978. The run consisted of 12 wins and 8 draws. The run ended with a 2-3 defeat at Coventry, on 23 December 1978.

- Coincidentally, a run of 18 League matches [and 22 games in all competitions] had ended nearly 12 months previously, on 26 December 1977, with a 2-6 home defeat by Manchester United.

- The club record for an unbeaten start to the League season is 19 matches, from the start of the 1978-79 season – see above.

- The longest unbeaten run, in all competitions is 28 matches, from 26 December 1984 to 8 May 1985 – consisting of 18 League, 6 FA Cup ties and 4 in the European Cup Winners' Cup. The run saw 24 wins, and 4 draws: Aston Villa and Manchester United in the League, Ipswich [FA Cup] and Bayern Munich in the Cup Winners' Cup.

- The best run of League results in the club's history was 16 wins and 2 draws in 18 games from 26 December 1984 to 8 May 1985. The 2 drawn matches in this period were both 1-1 draws at Aston Villa and Manchester United.

Home and away unbeaten sequences

- The longest unbeaten sequence of home League games is 39 matches from 16 September 1961 to 24 August 1963. The Blues also recorded 2 FA Cup wins, plus one Inter Cities Fairs Cup match, taking the run to 42 games without a home defeat.

- Season 1962-63 is the only time Everton have gone through a season without losing a single home match in the League – 14 wins, 7 draws and no defeats.

- The longest unbeaten sequence of away games is 10 League games from the start of the 1978-79 season and also 8 December 1984 to 4 May 1985.

- The latter sequence also contains the record for the most away games without defeat in all competitions, totalling 14 matches in all.

Sequences without a win

- The longest sequence without a League victory is 14 games from 6 March 1937 to 4 September 1937. The run consisted of 10 defeats and 4 draws.

- The post-War record is 13 League matches between 16 October and 25 December 1957.

- The longest sequence without a League home victory is 12 matches, between 16 October 1957 and 22 February 1958. Everton did win an FA Cup match during this period however.

- The longest sequence of away matches without recording a League win is 35 matches between 3 October 1970 and 4 April 1972. This was part of a run of 39 games without an away victory in all competitions, as the Blues failed to win a League Cup and FA Cup game away from home during this period, as well as 2 European Cup matches.

- The greatest number of League games without recording a victory from the start of the season is 12 matches in 1994-95.

Sequences of defeats

The Blues have lost 6 consecutive League matches on 5 occasions.

10 April 1929 – 4 May 1929
5 March 1930 – 12 April 1930
23 August 1958 – 9 September 1958
4 November 1972 – 9 December 1972
26 December 1996 – 19 January 1997

- The worst sequence of home League defeats at home is 7, between 4 April 1958 and 17 September 1958. Between 16 October 1957 and 17 September 1958, Everton played 21 home League matches and won just 2. Their home record during this period was: P 21 W 2 D8 L11 F27 A45.

- The Blues have lost a record 8 consecutive League matches away from home on 3 occasions, in 1921-22, 1948-49 and, most recently, 8 games were lost between 16 April 1994 and 22 October 1994.

- The worst losing sequence from the start of a season is 6 matches from the beginning of the 1958-59 campaign.

- Following a 3-0 reversal at Queens Park Rangers on 7 September 1985, Everton enjoyed a sequence of 323 League matches during which they lost only one match – a 2-6 defeat at Aston Villa, on 5 November 1989 – by more than a 2 goal margin. The run was ended by a 1-5 home defeat by Norwich on 25 September 1993.

- Everton lost consecutive home games 5-0 in the space of 4 days against Portsmouth and Birmingham City in September 1948. The preceding 2 matches were also defeats by 4-0, again by Portsmouth, and 1-0 by Middlesbrough. In 10 days Everton had lost 4 matches, scoring none, but conceding 15 goals.

Sequences of draws

- The record for consecutive drawn League matches is 5 between 15 October 1921 and 12 November 1921, and also between 4 May and 16 May 1977.

- Three consecutive goalless draws were played in League matches between 13 February and 27 February 1982. And again from 17 April to 4 May 1993.

Odd results and reversals

- On 25 December 1934, Everton defeated Sunderland 6-2 at Goodison Park but the return fixture the following day saw a 0-7 defeat at Roker Park!

- On 27 December 1955 Everton defeated Birmingham City 5-1 at Goodison Park but the previous day had seen Birmingham win 6-2 at St Andrews.

- A 14 day period in November 1959 saw Everton lose away at Newcastle 8-2, sandwiched between 2 home victories of 6-1, against Leicester City, and 4-0 against Birmingham.

- Both League matches against Leicester City in 1929-30 ended in 5-4 defeats for Everton.

- Everton lost both League matches against Manchester City in 1957-58 by 6-2 at Maine Road and 5-2 at Goodison.

- The last occasion Everton scored 5 times against the same side, both home and away in the same season, was in 1982-83, when they beat Luton 5-0 at Goodison and 5-1 at Kenilworth Road.

- Consecutive away League matches at Watford in 1983-84 and 1984-85, saw a 4-4 draw and a 5-4 win for Everton.

- When Everton lost 3-2 at home to Manchester United, on 9 September 1995 and 3-2 to Nottingham Forest 8 days later, it was the first time in their history that they had lost consecutive League matches by that scoreline.

- Everton pipped Wolverhamptom Wanderers for the League title in 1938-39, despite losing 7-0 at Molineux in the February of that season.

Winning from 2 goals down

- The last occasion Everton came from 2 goals behind to win a home game was famously on the last day of the 1993-94 season, when 2 goals from Graham Stuart and a rare Barry Horne goal saw them beat Wimbledon 3-2 at Goodison.

- The last occasion Everton came from 2 goals down to win, away from home, was when they defeated Ipswich Town 4-3 at Portman Road, on 16 November 1985.

- The 1985-86 season saw Everton 3 times recover from 2 goal deficits to win, against Bournemouth [League Cup] and Queens Park Rangers at home and Ipswich Town away.

Losing from 2 goals up

- The last occasion Everton were beaten at home after leading 2-0 was against Millwall, in the League Cup, on 4 October 1995. The Blues lost 4-2.

- The last occasion Everton lost an FA Cup tie after leading 2-0, was at home to Bolton in the 3rd Round in January 1994 – Mike Walker's first home game in charge of the club.

- The most recent instance of Everton losing away from home after leading by 2 goals, was the 3-2 loss at Tottenham Hotspur at White Hart Lane, on 5 September 2000.

- In the 1974-75 season, Everton lost at home to Carlisle and Sheffield United after leading 2-0 in both games. If they had won both matches, the Blues would have been champions. The Sheffield United game on 19 April 1975 was the last instance of Everton losing a League match at home after leading by 2 goals.

Other comebacks

- The last 2 occasions Everton have pulled back a 3 goal deficit to draw, have both been against Tottenham at White Hart Lane, in 3-3 draws on 30 October 1976 and 25 April 1992.

- In the League match against Watford, on 25 February 1984, Everton trailed by 0-2, 1-3 and 2-4 before a last minute goal by Adrian Heath earned a 4-4 draw. The next 4-4 draw in a League match was against Leeds United, on 24 October 1999, and was also courtesy of a last minute equaliser by David Weir.

GOALS

Leading goalscorers season by season

Leading Everton goalscorers for each season in the League and other games [FA Cup, League Cup and Europe].

Season	League goals		Others	
1888-89	E Chadwick	6	E Chadwick	6
1889-90	Geary	21	Geary	25
1890-91	Geary	20	Geary	20
1891-92	Latta	17	Latta	17
1892-93	Geary	19	Geary	23
1893-94	Southworth*	27	Southworth	27
1894-95	J Bell	15	J Bell	18
1895-96	Milward	17	Milward	19
1896-97	J Bell	15	J Bell	17
1897-98	L Bell	12	L Bell	15
1898-99	Proudfoot	12	Proudfoot	13
1899-00	Settle	10	Settle	10
1900-01	Taylor	11	Taylor	12
1901-02	Settle*	18	Settle	18
1902-03	Brearley	7	Brearley	8
1903-04	Young	10	Young	10
1904-05	Young	14	Young	14
1905-06	Young	12	Young	14
1906-07	Young*	28	Young	29
1907-08	Young	16	Young	21
1908-09	Freeman	38	Freeman	38
1909-10	Freeman	22	Freeman	26
1910-11	Young	8	Young	11
1911-12	Browell	12	Browell	19
1912-13	Browell	12	Browell	16
1913-14	Parker	17	Parker	17
1914-15	Parker*	36	Parker	38
1919-20	Kirsopp	14	Kirsopp	14
1920-21	Crossley	15	Crossley	18
1921-22	Fazackerley	12	Fazackerley	12
1922-23	W Chadwick, Williams	13	W Chadwick, Williams	13
1923-24	W Chadwick*	28	W Chadwick	30
1924-25	Broad	8	W Chadwick	9
1925-26	Dean	32	Dean	33
1926-27	Dean	21	Dean	24
1927-28	Dean*	60	Dean	63
1928-29	Dean	26	Dean	26
1929-30	Dean	23	Dean	25

*indicates leading scorer in division that season

Season	League goals		Others	
1930-31	Dean	39	Dean	48
1931-32	Dean*	45	Dean	46
1932-33	Dean	24	Dean	29
1933-34	White	14	White	14
1934-35	Dean	26	Dean	27
1935-36	Cunliffe	23	Cunliffe	23
1936-37	Dean	24	Dean	27
1937-38	Lawton*	28	Lawton	28
1938-39	Lawton*	34	Lawton	38
1946-47	Dodds	17	Dodds	17
1947-48	Dodds	13	Dodds	14
1948-49	Wainwright	10	Wainwright	10
1949-50	Wainwright	11	Wainwright	13
1950-51	McIntosh	11	McIntosh	11
1951-52	Parker	15	Parker	16
1952-53	Eglington	14	Parker	17
1953-54	Parker	31	Parker	33
1954-55	Parker	19	Parker	19
1955-56	J Harris	19	J Harris	21
1956-57	McNamara	10	McNamara	10
1957-58	Thomas	15	Thomas, J Harris	15
1958-59	Hickson	17	Hickson	22
1959-60	Collins	14	Collins	14
1960-61	Vernon	21	Vernon	22
1961-62	Vernon	26	Vernon	28
1962-63	Vernon	24	Vernon	27
1963-64	Vernon	18	Vernon	20
1964-65	Pickering	27	Pickering	37
1965-66	Pickering	18	Pickering	22
1966-67	Ball	15	Ball	18
1967-68	Ball	20	Ball, Royle	20
1968-69	Royle	22	Royle	29
1969-70	Royle	23	Royle	23
1970-71	Royle	17	Royle	23
1971-72	Johnson, Royle	9	Johnson	11
1972-73	Connolly, Harper, Royle	7	Harper	8
1973-74	Lyons	9	Lyons	9
1974-75	Latchford	17	Latchford	19
1975-76	Latchford	12	Latchford	13
1976-77	Latchford	17	Latchford	25
1977-78	Latchford*	30	Latchford	32
1978-79	King	12	Latchford	20
1979-80	Kidd	10	Kidd	18

*indicates leading scorer in division that season

Season	League goals		Others	
1980-81	Eastoe	15	Eastoe	19
1981-82	Sharp	15	Sharp	15
1982-83	Sharp	15	Sharp	17
1983-84	Heath	12	Heath	18
1984-85	Sharp	21	Sharp	30
1985-86	Lineker*	30	Lineker	38
1986-87	Steven	14	Steven	15
1987-88	Sharp	13	Sharp	20
1988-89	Cottee	13	Cottee	15
1989-90	Cottee	13	Cottee	15
1990-91	Cottee	10	Cottee	16
1991-92	Beardsley	15	Beardsley	19
1992-93	Cottee	12	Cottee	13
1993-94	Cottee	16	Cottee	19
1994-95	Rideout	14	Rideout	16
1995-96	Kanchelskis	16	Kanchelskis	16
1996-97	Ferguson	10	Ferguson, Speed	11
1997-98	Ferguson	11	Ferguson	11
1998-99	Campbell	9	Campbell	9
1999-00	Campbell	12	Campbell	12
2000-01	Campbell	9	Campbell	10

*Indicates leading scorer in division that season

Leading goalscorer on most occasions [League only]

Dixie Dean	10
Alex Young [1901 – 1911]	6
Joe Royle, Tony Cottee	5

Leading goalscorer on most occasions [all games]

Dixie Dean	10
Alex Young [1901 – 1911]	6
Bob Latchford, Tony Cottee	5

Leading goalscorers, in all major domestic and European competitions

	League	Other	Total
Dixie Dean	349	28	377
Graeme Sharp	111	39	150
Bob Latchford	106	32	138
Alex Young [1901 –1911]	110	15	125
Joe Royle	102	17	119
Dave Hickson	95	16	111
Edgar Chadwick	97	13	110
Roy Vernon	101	9	110
Jimmy Settle	84	13	97
Alfred Millward	85	11	96
Kevin Sheedy	67	26	93
Alex Stevenson	82	8	90
John W Parker	82	7	89
Adrian Heath	71	18	89
Alex Young [1960 – 1968]	77	10	87
Tony Cottee	72	15	87
Fred Geary	78	8	86
Tommy Eglington	76	6	82
Derek Temple	72	10	82
Jack Sharp	68	12	80
Jack Taylor	66	14	80
Alan Ball	66	12	78
Jimmy Cunliffe	73	3	76
Eddie Wainwright	68	8	76
Jimmy Harris	65	7	72
Bobby Parker	68	3	71
Alex Latta	69	1	70
Tommy Lawton	65	5	70
John Bell	62	8	70
Fred Pickering	56	14	70

Number of games required to reach 100 goals

The number of games it took the top 8 Everton players to score 100 goals – in all competitions.

Dixie Dean	105 games
Roy Vernon	173 games
Bob Latchford	192 games
Joe Royle	202 games
Dave Hickson	217 games
Alex Young [1901 – 1911]	219 games
Edgar Chadwick	258 games
Graeme Sharp	263 games

Number of League matches required to reach 100 goals

Only 6 players have achieved this feat.

Dixie Dean	104 League games
Roy Vernon	176 League games
Bob Latchford	212 League games
Alex Young [1901 – 1911]	217 League games
Joe Royle	226 League games
Graeme Sharp	257 League games

- Roy Vernon scored his 100th League goal in his final League game for the club, against Aston Villa, on 13 March 1965.

- Of the 8 players who have scored 100 or more goals for the club, only Bob Latchford and Joe Royle [9 games] and Bob Latchford and Graeme Sharp [2 games] have appeared in the same side. The former pair's goals in a 3-2 win at West Ham, on 24 August 1974, provides the only instance of 2 of the 8 players with 100 goals or more for the club, scoring in the same game.

- Tony Cottee scored the 100th League goal of his career against Spurs, for Everton, on 3 December 1988. The first League goal of his career, and his 200th, were also against Tottenham.

- In the 1927-28 season, Dixie Dean scored against 19 out of the 21 League clubs, apart from West Ham and Sunderland.

Top scorers

The following table compares the goalscoring record of Dixie Dean with the 4 post-War players who have scored 100 or more League goals.

	Dean	Vernon	Royle	Latchford	Sharp
Goals	349	101	102	106	111
Home	230	62	69	59	68
Away	119	39	33	47	43
% Home	66%	61%	68%	56%	62%
% Away	34%	39%	32%	44%	38%
Goals	349	101	102	106	111
All Everton goals	849	375	331	346	496
% of all Everton goals	41%	27%	31%	31%	22%

The above tables show how 'Big Bob' scored a high proportion of goals away from home [anybody above 40% is unusual] and what a dominant force Dean was. He scored 41% of Everton's goals in the games he played.

Everton players who have scored a goal in at least every other game

These 13 Everton players have each scored more than 25 goals, in all competitions, during their Everton career, and have a goal ratio of at least 1 in 2.

	Goals	Games	Goal ratio per game
Jack Southworth	36	32	1.13
Fred Geary	86	98	0.88
Dixie Dean	377	431	0.87
Bobby Parker	71	92	0.77
Tommy Lawton	70	95	0.74
Gary Lineker	38	52	0.73
Bertie Freeman	67	94	0.71
Jock Dodds	37	58	0.64
Tom Browell	37	60	0.62
Fred Pickering	70	115	0.61
Roy Vernon	110	200	0.55
John W Parker	89	176	0.51
Wilf Chadwick	55	109	0.50

Most goals in a season
Progressive record for players with most goals in a season, all in Division 1.

6	Edgar Chadwick	1888-89
21	Fred Geary	1889-90
27	Jack Southworth	1893-94
28	Alex Young	1906-07
38	Bertie Freeman	1908-09
60	Dixie Dean	1927-28

● The tallies for Bertie Freeman and Dixie Dean were League records at the time.

● Jack Southworth was the first player to be leading scorer in the 1st Division with different clubs: Blackburn in 1890-91 and Everton in 1893-94.

30 or more League goals in a season

Bertie Freeman	38	1908-09
Bobby Parker	36	1914-15
Dixie Dean	32	1925-26
Dixie Dean	60	1927-28
Dixie Dean	39	1930-31 [Division 2]
Dixie Dean	45	1931-32
Tommy Lawton	34	1938-39
John W Parker	31	1953-54 [Division 2]
Bob Latchford	30	1977-78
Gary Lineker	30	1985-86

● Bob Latchford and Gary Lineker are the only Everton post-War players to top the goalscoring list in the English top-flight.

● Bob Latchford's 30 League goal season of 1977-78 won him £10,000 from a national newspaper. Echoing the feat of Dixie Dean in 1927-28, 'Big Bob' achieved the magic figure by scoring twice against Chelsea at Goodison, on the final day of the season.

● The last player to achieve 20 League goals in a season was Gary Lineker as above. The greatest number of League goals in a season since then, was the 16 scored by Tony Cottee in 1993-94 and Andrei Kanchelskis in 1995-96.

● Kevin Campbell was the Blue's leading scorer in the League, with 9 goals in 1998-99, after making his first appearance just 8 games from the end of the season!

● The record for the most goals in a season by a defender is held by Derek Mountfield, whose contribution to the triumphant 1984-85 season was a staggering 14 goals in 57 games – not one from the penalty spot.

Leading scorers – decade by decade

Everton's leading scorers in the League, for each decade, are listed below.

1888 – 1899	Edgar Chadwick	97
1900 – 1909	Alex Young	102
1910 – 1919	Bobby Parker	54
1920 – 1929	Dixie Dean	157
1930 – 1939	Dixie Dean	192
1940 – 1949	Eddie Wainwright	39
1950 – 1959	Dave Hickson	95
1960 – 1969	Roy Vernon	101
1970 – 1979	Bob Latchford	99
1980 – 1989	Graeme Sharp	103
1990 – 1999	Tony Cottee	56

Most goals in a game

The following players have scored more than 4 goals in a single match [all League games unless stated] for the club.

Jack Southworth	6	v West Bromwich Albion [h]	30 December 1893
Dixie Dean	5	v Manchester United [h]	8 October 1927
Dixie Dean	5	v Sheffield Wednesday [h]	17 October 1931
Dixie Dean	5	v Chelsea [h]	14 November 1931
Tommy Eglington	5	v Doncaster Rovers [h]	27 September 1952 [Div 2]
Bob Latchford	5	v Wimbledon [h]	29 August 1978 [League Cup]

- Jack Southworth's 6 goals in a single match was the first such instance in League history. In May 1890 he was the first player to score 5 times in a League match, when playing for Blackburn Olympic.
- The last Everton player to score 4 times in a League match was Graeme Sharp, at Southampton, on 3 October 1987.
- The last 4-goal, home League performance, was Joe Royle's, in the 8-0 win against Southampton on 20 November 1971. Curiously, this was the same day as Ted McDougall's record-breaking 9 goals in a single game, in the FA Cup, for Bournemouth against Margate.

Prolific spells

- Dixie Dean set a club record when scoring in 12 consecutive League matches in Division 2 from 6 December 1930 to 18 February 1931. In this sequence he scored 23 goals, with two 4-goal tallies and a hat trick. The previous record had been held by Bertie Freeman, with 17 goals in 10 consecutive League matches from 10 October 1908 to 12 December 1908, a club record in the top-flight that still stands today.

- The post-War League scoring record is held by Bob Latchford, who scored in 7 consecutive League matches, from 29 November 1975 to 27 December 1975.

- In all competitions, the post-War scoring record is 8 consecutive matches [6 League, 2 FA Cup] held by Dave Hickson between 23 January 1954 and 6 March 1954.

- The greatest number of consecutive League games scored in from the start of the season is 6, jointly held by Fred Geary [1890-91], Dixie Dean [1933-34] and Tommy Lawton [1938-39].

Other prolific scoring periods in the League

These goalscorers had prolific spells, although not involving a goal in every game.

Jack Southworth	16 goals in 7 games	1893-94
Bobby Parker	19 goals in 11 games	1914-15
Dixie Dean	17 goals in 9 games	1927-28 [August 27 – October 8]
Dixie Dean	23 goals in 12 games	1927-28 – 1928-29
Dixie Dean	23 goals in 12 games	1931-32
Bob Latchford	16 goals in 12 games	1977-78
Gary Lineker	13 goals in 10 games	1985-86

- The record for scoring for Everton in consecutive seasons is jointly held by Jack Taylor, who scored at least one goal in 14 consecutive seasons from 1896 – 1910 [although his last season was a goal in the FA Cup only], and Dixie Dean, who scored at least one League goal in every season from 1924 – 1938.

- The post-War record is held by Dave Watson, who scored at least one goal for the club in 11 consecutive seasons from 1986 – 1997. The only other post-War player with at least one goal in 10 consecutive seasons, is Graeme Sharp from 1981 – 1991.

Goalscoring over 3 decades

Only 2 players have scored for the club in 3 different decades.

	First	Last
Jack Taylor	5 September 1896	19 January 1910
Jack Sharp	14 October 1899	6 April 1910

Debut goalscorers

The following players have scored on their first-team debuts for Everton, all being League matches unless otherwise stated.

G Fleming [2]	v Accrington Stanley [h]	8 September 1888
R Watson	v Aston Villa [a]	22 September 1888
J Costley [2]	v Derby County [a]	20 October 1888
W Brown	v Bolton Wanderers [h]	3 November 1888
Coyne	v Burnley [h]	24 November 1888
Fred Geary [2]	v Blackburn Rovers [h]	7 September 1889
Charlie Parry	v Blackburn Rovers [h]	7 September 1889
Orr	v Derby County [a]	5 October 1889
A Brady [2]	v Stoke City [h]	2 November 1889
W Campbell	v West Bromwich Albion [a]	6 September 1890
Jack Southworth	v Derby County [a]	9 September 1893
J Walker	v Aston Villa [h]	16 September 1893
H Reay	v Bolton Wanderers [a]	16 April 1894
T McInnes	v Sheffield Wednesday [h]	1 September 1894
W Williams	v Stoke City [h]	7 January 1895
A Flewitt	v Nottingham Forest [h]	7 September 1895
Jack Taylor	v Sheffield Wednesday [h]	5 September 1896
L Bell [2]	v Bolton Wanderers [h]	4 September 1897
J Divers	v Derby County [a]	11 September 1897
J Proudfoot	v Blackburn Rovers [h]	1 September 1898
W Oldham	v Stoke City [h]	10 December 1898
Harold Hardman	v Blackburn Rovers [h]	1 September 1903
F Oliver [3]	v Nottingham County [h]	14 October 1905
H Cook	v Blackburn Rovers [a]	17 March 1906
H Mountford	v Nottingham Forest [h]	2 November 1907
G Barlow	v Middlesbrough [a]	19 September 1908
R Turner	v Liverpool [h]	9 April 1909
J Gourlay	v Chelsea [h]	19 March 1910
L Weller	v Blackburn Rovers [a]	11 April 1910
E Magner	v Preston [a]	7 January 1911
A Burton	v Tottenham Hotspur [h]	2 September 1911
Tom Browell [2]	v Manchester United [h]	6 January 1912
S Simms	v Blackburn Rovers [a]	26 December 1912
T Page	v Middlesbrough [h]	4 October 1913
Joe Clennell	v Aston Villa [h]	24 January 1914
W Kirsopp	v Tottenham Hotspur [h]	1 January 1915
T Mayson	v Chelsea [h]	30 August 1919
J Kearslake	v Oldham Athletic [a]	28 February 1920
S Davies	v Manchester City [h]	5 February 1921
Jack Cock	v Stoke City [h]	20 January 1923

D Murray	v Cardiff City [a]	5 September 1925
Dick Forshaw	v Newcastle United [a]	5 March 1927
A Weldon	v Leeds United [h]	12 March 1927
Albert Geldard	v Middlesbrough [a]	19 November 1932
Nat Cunliffe	v Aston Villa [a]	25 March 1933
C Leyfield	v Leicester City [h]	29 August 1934
W Hartill	v Portsmouth [h]	11 September 1935
Stan Bentham [2]	v Grimsby [a]	23 November 1935
Robert Bell	v Leeds United [a]	18 April 1936
Tommy Lawton	v Wolverhampton Wanderers [a]	13 February 1937
Jock Dodds	v Grimsby [h]	2 November 1946
Aubrey Powell	v Newcastle United [h]	21 August 1948
James McIntosh	v Blackpool [h]	5 March 1949
Derek Mayers	v Bury [h]	15 April 1953
William Haughey	v Manchester City [a]	19 April 1957
Jack Keeley	v Bolton Wanderers [a]	26 December 1957
Bobby Collins	v Manchester City [a]	13 September 1958
Robert Laverick	v West Bromwich Albion [h]	15 February 1959
Frank Wignall	v Burnley [h]	2 September 1959
Barry Rees	v West Ham United [a]	19 October 1963
Fred Pickering [3]	v Nottingham Forest [h]	14 March 1964
Alan Ball	v Fulham [a]	20 August 1966
David Johnson	v Burnley [a]	9 January 1971
Mike Lyons	v Nottingham Forest [a]	20 March 1971
Ross Jack	v Middlesbrough [a]	6 March 1979
Joe McBride	v Bolton Wanderers [a]	26 December 1979
Alan Ainscow	v Birmingham City [h]	29 August 1981
Alan Biley	v Birmingham City [h]	29 August 1981
Rob Wakenshaw	v Manchester United [h]	5 May 1984
Ian Wilson	v Rotherham United [h] [League Cup]	22 September 1987
Tony Cottee [3]	v Newcastle United [h]	27 August 1988
David Unsworth	v Tottenham Hotspur [a]	25 April 1992
Barry Horne	v Sheffield Wednesday [h]	15 August 1992
Gary Speed	v Newcastle United [h]	17 August 1996
Michael Madar	v Crystal Palace [a]	10 January 1998

Debut goalscorers

- Contrary to many publications, Fred Pickering [v Nottingham Forest 1963-64] and Tony Cottee [v Newcastle 1988-89] are not the only players to score hat tricks on their club debut, F Oliver scored 3 times on his first appearance for the club against Nottingham County on 14 October 1905.

- David Johnson scored for the club on his Youth Cup, Central League, League, FA Cup, League Cup and European debuts. He also scored on his Merseyside derby debut and on his England debut in 1975, whilst with Ipswich Town.

- Ross Jack is the only post-War player to have scored on his sole first team appearance, doing so in the 2-1 win at Middlesbrough on 6 March 1979.

- Everton never lost any of the 18 matches in which Andy Gray scored for the club.

Goalscoring – team records

Record scoring sequences in League matches.

2 matches – 15 goals

8-1	Sheffield Wednesday [h]	23 December 1893
7-1	West Bromwich Albion [h]	30 December 1893

3 matches – 20 goals

9-3	Sheffield Wednesday [h]	17 October 1931
3-2	Aston Villa [a]	24 October 1931
8-1	Newcastle United [h]	31 October 1931
6-2	Derby County [a]	13 February 1954
6-1	Brentford [h]	24 February 1954
8-4	Plymouth Argyle [h]	27 February 1954

4 Matches – 25 goals

5-1	Sheffield United [a]	10 October 1931
9-3	Sheffield Wednesday [h]	17 October 1931
3-2	Aston Villa [a]	24 October 1931
8-1	Newcastle United [h]	31 October 1931

- In addition to the above sequences, 13 consecutive League and Cup matches in the 1930-31 season, from 27 December to 28 February, saw 60 goals scored: 9-1, 3-2, 5-2, 2-0, 2-1, 6-0, 3-1, 4-2, 7-0, 5-3, 5-2 and 9-1.

- Adrian Heath's winning goal against Aston Villa, on 13 October 1984, set up a club record run of scoring 15 League goals without reply: 2-1 Aston Villa [h], 1-0 Liverpool [a], 5-0 Manchester United [h], 3-0 Leicester City [h], 1-0 West Ham [a] and 4-0 Stoke City [h]. The run ended with a 4-2 defeat at Norwich City.

Most League goals in a season

Everton have scored 100 or more League goals in a season on 3 occasions.

121   1930-31 [Division 2]
116   1931-32
102   1927-28

- Each of the above seasons had 42 games; the best seasonal goals-per-game ratio is 3 goals per game, when 90 League goals were scored in 30 matches in 1893-94.
- The post-War record for League goals in a season is 92, in the promotion year from Division 2 in 1953-54.
- The post-War record in the top-flight, is the 88 League goals scored in 1961-62 and 1984-85.
- The record for League goals scored in home matches is 84 in 1931-32 and away from home League, is 45 goals in 1930-31.
- The highest number of goals, in all competitions, scored in a season is the 143 scored in 1930-31 – 121 goals in the League and 22 in the FA Cup.
- The post-War record for the highest number of goals, in all competitions is 124, in 1984-85 – 88 League, 12 FA Cup, 8 League Cup and 16 European Cup Winners' Cup.

Fewest scoreless games

- Since 1905, when the season was extended to 38 games, the least number of League games in which the Blues have failed to score in the season is just 2, during the 1930-31 Division 2, title-winning season.
- The post-War record is 4, set in 1984-85. During that season, Everton scored in 26 consecutive domestic League and Cup matches, from 15 December 1984 onwards.
- The Blues scored in every League game [40 in total] during a 12 month period from 15 March 1929.

Seasons in which Everton have failed to score 4 goals in a single game

Season	Best result
2000-01	3-0
1981-82	3-0
1972-73	3-1
1924-25	3-1

- The 1981-82 season is unique in that it is the only season in the club's history where either side failed to score 4 or more goals in a game involving Everton.

Fewest goals in a season

- The fewest goals scored in a League season is when just 37 goals were totalled in 1971-72. Things would have been worse but for the 8-0 win against Southampton!

- Just 21 League goals – an all time record – were scored at home in the 1983-84 season. The first 11 home games saw just 5 goals scored. Only 4 out of 21 home games saw the Blues scoring more than once.

- The record for the fewest League goals away from home is the 8 goals scored in 1948-49 – the Blues taking 9 matches before scoring away from home for the first time.

- Everton failed to score in a record 19 League games in 1948-49, 1971-72 and 1993-94.

- The club record for most consecutive League games without a goal is 6, in both 1950-51 and 1993-94.

- Only 11 goals were scored in the opening 21 League games of the 1983-84 season, with just one game, a 2-1 win at Spurs, seeing 2 goals scored by the Blues.

- The first 23 League games of the 1998-99 season produced just 12 goals, with 4 of the first 5 home League matches resulting in goalless draws. Goodison had to wait until 31 October for the first Everton player to score at home in the season – a Craig Short own goal against Manchester United!

Goals conceded

- The highest number of League goals conceded in a season was 92, in the 1929-30 season. 5 goals in a single game were conceded on 4 occasions and 4 goals in 6 matches.

- The post-War record is the 87 goals let in during the 1958-59 season. The club conceded 38 goals in the first 12 games of the season, with the biggest post-War home and away defeats occurring in the space of 5 weeks – Arsenal 1-6 and Spurs 4-10.

- The least number of goals conceded in a League season occurred in 1987-88, when just 27 goals were scored against the Blues in 40 games. The record for a 42-game season is the 31 goals let in during the 1986-87 title year.

- A post-War club record of just 11 goals was conceded at home in the 1986-87 season. 12 clean sheets were kept in 21 home games. The 10 goals conceded in 19 games in 1906-07 remains the record.

- The club record for consecutive clean sheets is 7 matches, between November 1 and December 17 1994. Strangely, Mike Walker was sacked as manager, just 2 games into this sequence. New manager, Joe Royle, saw his side keep 5 clean sheets before the 4-1 home defeat by Sheffield Wednesday, on Boxing Day. The total time without conceding a goal was 12 hours 15 minutes.

Different goalscorers

- The highest number of different goalscorers in a League season is 17, set in 1919-20, and equalled in 1992-93. The fewest is the 7 players, who scored in 1923-24, when 52 of the Blues 62 goals were scored by just 3 players [Chadwick, Cock and Irvine].

- In the post-War era, the lowest number of different goalscorers was the 9 players in 1951-52 and, surprisingly, the 9 in 1969-70, when the Blues were the League champions.

- A record 6 different players scored in the 8-3 win over Cardiff City on 28 April 1962: Vernon [3], Bingham, Gabriel, Stevens, Temple and Young.

- A Football League record was set against Charlton, on 7 February 1931, when all 5 Everton forwards scored in a 19 minute spell, Jimmy Stein scored in the 19th minute and he was followed by Dean [22], Dunn [27], Critchley [30] and Johnson [36]. The Blues ran out 7-0 winners.

- In 16 League games between 17 November 1984 and 30 March 1985, 8 players scored twice in a match for Everton – Heath, Sharp, Mountfield, Steven, Sheedy, Stevens, Gray and Richardson.

Under 18 goalsorers

Players under 18 who have scored for Everton since the War.

17 years 137 days	Alan Tyrer	v Leeds United [h]	23 April 1960
17 years 203 days	Herbert Llewellyn	v Bolton [h]	25 August 1956
17 years 344 days	Danny Cadamarteri	v Barnsley [h]	20 September 1997
17 years 360 days	Michael Ball	v Arsenal [h]	27 September 1997

- Although Joe Royle is the club's youngest post-War player, he was 18 years 12 days when he scored his first goal for the club on 19 April 1967.
- Pre-War records are sketchy, although Tommy Lawton was 17 years 132 days when he scored on his debut against Wolves on 13 February 1937.
- Francis Jeffers is the club's youngest post-War scorer in the FA Cup, being 18 years 20 days when he scored against Coventry, on 13 February 1999.
- The youngest debutant goalscorer in the post-War era is Herbert Llewellyn, as shown above.
- The youngest post-War hat trick scorer is Joe Royle, who was 19 years 237 days when he scored 3 times against Leicester City, on 30 November 1968. He remains the only teenager to achieve this feat since 1945.
- Dixie Dean was 18 years 269 days when he scored his first hat trick against Burnley, on 17 October 1925. Tommy Lawton was 19 years 31 days when he scored a hat trick against Middlesbrough, on 5 November 1938.

The club's oldest post-War scorers

Wally Fielding	v WBA [a]	27 September 1958	38 years 305 days
Richard Gough	v Wimbledon [h]	21 August 1999	37 years 138 days
Dave Watson	v Huddersfield [a]*	15 September 1998	36 years 299 days

[*League Cup]

- The oldest hat trick scorer is Jock Dodds, who was 33 years 19 days when he scored 3 goals against Preston, on 25 September 1948.

Quick scoring

- David Johnson scored with his first touch less than 20 seconds after coming on as a substitute against Watford, at Goodison, on 15 January 1983. He also holds the record for the quickest goal, at any level, in the club's history: 5 seconds in a Youth Cup game.

- Howard Kendall scored after just 14 seconds of the 5-2 home win over Chelsea, on 28 March 1970.

- Tony Cottee scored after 34 seconds into his Blues debut against Newcastle United on 27 August 1988.

- Dixie Dean scored 5 goals in 32 minutes in the 7-2 win over Chelsea, on 14 November 1931.

- The quickest goal conceded by Everton is probably when Chris Sutton scored after just 13 seconds for Blackburn Rovers, at Goodison, on 1 April 1995.

- John McIntyre scored 4 goals in 5 minutes for Blackburn Rovers against Everton on 16 September 1922.

Penalties

Everton players who have scored 10 or more penalties since the War.

Trevor Steven	19 goals	21 attempts
David Unsworth	16 goals	19 attempts
Roy Vernon	15 goals	16 attempts
TE Jones	12 goals	18 attempts
Joe Royle	11 goals	15 attempts
Graeme Sharp	10 goals	13 attempts
Alan Ball	10 goals	15 attempts

- Peter Beardsley has the best record of any post-War player, with 6 penalties out of 6 attempts, although he did miss for Newcastle at Goodison in 1986!

The 3 most recent instances of players scoring 2 penalties in a game

Trevor Steven	v Luton Town [h]	9 May 1987
David Unsworth	v Tottenham Hotspur [a]	14 August 1999
David Unsworth	v Birmingham City [h] [FA Cup]	8 January 2000

- The record for the greatest number of successful penalties in a season is held by Trevor Steven who, in 1986-87, scored 10 penalties in League games and one in the League Cup.

- High profile misses include Trevor Steven [v Arsenal] and Duncan McKenzie [v Bolton] in League Cup Semi Finals. However, the most infamous miss in the club's history was at Maine Road in the 1953 FA Cup Semi Final against Bolton, when Tommy Clinton fired wide, which meant that the Blues were unable to force a 4-4 draw, after being 4-0 down at half time.

- Joe Harper [v Spurs, December 1972] and John Collins [v Aston Villa, August 1998] both missed penalties on their debuts for the club.

- Ken Barnes for Manchester City against Everton, on 7 December 1957, provides the most recent instance of a player scoring a hat trick of penalties in the English top-flight.

- David Unsworth scored 9 times in the 1999-00 season with the help of 7 penalties.

Own goals by Everton players since 1969-70

Twenty-six Everton players have suffered the ignominy of scoring in their own net since the start of the 1969-70 campaign. Whilst Sandy Brown's effort remains the most famous, others will be remembered as serial own goal offenders! All matches are in the League, unless otherwise stated.

Sandy Brown	v Liverpool [h]	6 December 1969
Gordon West	v Keflavik [h] [European Cup]	16 September 1970
Tommy Wright	v Newcastle United [h]	24 October 1970
Howard Kendall	v West Ham United [h]	30 March 1971
Tommy Wright	v Crystal Palace [a]	1 May 1971
Tommy Wright	v Liverpool [a]	4 March 1972
John McLaughlin	v Liverpool [a]	4 March 1972
Tommy Wright	v Manchester City [h]	11 March 1972
Mike Lyons	v Stoke City [a]	22 April 1972
Henry Newton	v Manchester City [h]	11 November 1972
Tommy Wright	v Leicester City [h]	27 January 1973
John McLaughlin	v Norwich City[a]	17 November 1973
Terry Darracott	v Stoke City [a]	8 November 1975
Ken McNaught	v Aston Villa [a]	22 November 1975
Dave Clements	v Ipswich Town [h]	6 December 1975
Roger Kenyon	v Manchester United [a]	17 April 1976
Mike Lyons	v Aston Villa [h]	28 August 1976
Ken McNaught	v West Ham United [h]	23 October 1976
Martin Dobson	v West Ham United [a]	24 September 1977
Trevor Ross	v Manchester United [h]	26 December 1977
Mike Lyons	v Liverpool [a]	20 October 197x9
Mike Lyons	v Sunderland [a]	16 August 1980
John Bailey	v Liverpool [a]	21 March 1981
Gary Stevens	v West Ham United [a]	27 November 1982
John Bailey	v Norwich City [h]	26 November 1983
Derek Mountfield	v Watford [a]	29 September 1984
Gary Stevens	v Sheffield Wednesday [h]	28 December 1985
Pat Van Den Hauwe	v Blackburn Rovers [h] [FA Cup]	25 January 1986
Derek Mountfield	v Watford [h]	25 October 1986
Kevin Ratcliffe	v Charlton [a]	10 April 1989
Mike Newell	v Southampton [a]	16 March 1991
Martin Keown	v Leeds United [h]	23 February 1992

Dave Watson	v Leeds United [a]	30 April 1994
Gary Ablett	v Wimbledon [h]	7 May 1994
Andy Hinchcliffe	v Nottingham Forest [h]	30 August 1994
Dave Watson	v Nottingham Forest [a]	17 September 1995
David Unsworth	v Manchester United [a]	21 August 1996
Craig Short	v Southampton [a]	5 March 1997
Claus Thomsen	v Liverpool [h]	16 April 1997
Dave Watson	v West Ham United [h]	23 August 1997
Slaven Bilic	v Arsenal [a]	3 May 1998
Craig Short	v Manchester United [h]	30 October 1998
Dave Watson	v Tottenham Hotspur [h]	15 January 2000
Steve Watson	v Middlesbrough [a]	9 September 2000
Gary Naysmith	v Manchester City [a]	9 December 2000
Steve Watson	v Manchester United [a]	3 February 2001
David Unsworth	v Newcastle United [h]	3 March 2001

- Tommy Wright has scored the most own-goals, with 5, followed by Mike Lyons and Dave Watson who have each scored 4.

- The most recent instance of 2 Everton players scoring own goals in the same game, occurred in the derby match, on 4 March 1972, when both Tommy Wright and John McLaughlin put through their own net.

- In the 1971-72 season, Tommy Wright scored own goals on consecutive Saturdays, after just 35 seconds of the derby at Anfield, and then against Manchester City at Goodison seven days later, he put through his own net after just 32 seconds.

- The last Everton keeper credited with scoring an own goal is Gordon West, against Keflavik, in1970.

- Derek Mountfield scored 2 own goals in his Everton career, both were against Watford and in both games he also scored at the right end!

Own goals by opposing players

Players who have scored own goals for teams in matches involving Everton since 1969-70.

Mel Blyth	Crystal Palace [a]	25 September 1971
Graham Cross	Leicester City [a]	9 September 1972
Gary Sprake	Birmingham City [a]	27 October 1973
Duncan Forbes	Norwich City [a]	17 November 1973
Archie Styles	Birmingham City [a]	18 January 1975
Mick Horswill	Manchester City [a]	8 February 1975
Phil Parkes	Queens Park Rangers [a]	21 August 1976
Don Gillies	Bristol City [a]	5 March 1977
Kenny Burns	Nottingham Forest [h] [League Cup]	7 November 1978
Sam Irvine	Stoke City [a]	6 September 1979
Paul Hart	Leeds United [h]	13 November 1979
Kenny Sansom	Arsenal [h] [FA Cup]	3 January 1981
Byron Stevenson	Swansea City [a]	16 October 1982
John Wark	Ipswich Town [h]	14 May 1983
Colin Griffin	Shrewsbury [h] [FA Cup]	18 February 1984
John Gidman	Manchester United [a] [League Cup]	30 October 1984
Darren Hughes	Shrewsbury [a] [League Cup]	29 October 1985
Mal Donaghy	Luton Town [a] [FA Cup]	8 March 1986
James Mullen	Newport City [a]	7 October 1986
John O'Neill	Leicester City [h]	28 December 1986
Mark Wright	Southampton [h]	14 March 1987
Joe McLaughlin	Chelsea [a]	4 April 1987
Terry Fenwick	Tottenham Hotspur [a]	9 March 1988
Alan McLeary	Millwall [a]	17 September 1988
Paul McGrath	Aston Villa [a]	5 November 1989
Tony Cascarino	Aston Villa [h]	5 May 1990
John Pemberton	Sheffield United [a] [League Cup]	30 October 1990
Jason Cundy	Chelsea [a]	1 January 1991
Paul Stewart	Tottenham Hotspur [a]	24 April 1991
Stuart Pearce	Notts Forest [a]	17 August 1991
Ian Brightwell	Manchester City [h]	31 October 1992
Colin Hendry	Blackburn Rovers [h]	3 March 1993
Phil Whelan	Ipswich [a]	30 October 1993

Eric Young	Crystal Palace [a] [League Cup]	10 November 1993
Alan McDonald	Queens Park Rangers [a]	18 March 1995
David Wetherall	Leeds United [h]	30 December 1995
Andrew O'Brien	Bradford City [h] [FA Cup]	25 January 1997
Neil Ruddock	Liverpool [h]	18 October 1997
Michael Duberry	Chelsea [h]	18 January 1998
Jaap Stam	Manchester United [h]	8 August 1999
Claus Lundekvam	Southampton [h]	21 August 1999

Most recent occurrences of Everton players scoring at both ends

Derek Mountfield	v Watford [a]	29 September 1984
Pat Van Den Hauwe	v Blackburn Rovers [h]	25 January 1986 [FA Cup]
Derek Mountfield	v Watford [h]	25 October 1986
Mike Newell	v Southampton [a]	16 March 1991
David Unsworth	v Newcastle United [h]	3 March 2001

- Archie Styles made 27 appearances for Everton from 1972 to 1974 without scoring, but he put through his own goal for Birmingham City against the Blues at St Andrews on 18 January 1975. This is the last instance of a former Everton player scoring an own goal against the club in a League match.

- Former Everton player, John Gidman, [Manchester United in 1984] and Darren Hughes [Shrewsbury in 1985] have both scored own goals in League Cup ties against the Blues.

- Although famously credited with throwing the ball into the net at the Kop end at Anfield in his Leeds days, keeper, Gary Sprake, also conceded an own goal whilst playing for Birmingham City against Everton, on 27 October 1973.

Scoring droughts

The following outfield players made over 100 appearances for Everton without scoring a single goal in their career at the club [figures in brackets are the number of League games included].

John McDonald	1920 – 1927	224	[208]
Robert Balmer	1902 – 1912	188	[165]
Eric Moore	1949 – 1957	184	[171]
William Brown	1914 – 1928	179	[170]
Terry Darracott	1967 – 1979	172	[148]
Ray Wilson	1964 – 1969	143	[116]
Jimmy Tansey	1953 – 1959	142	[133]
George Saunders	1946 – 1952	140	[133]
Ben Williams	1929 – 1936	139	[131]
David Raitt	1922 – 1928	131	[122]
Jack Crelley	1899 – 1807	127	[116]
W Stevenson	1907 – 1914	125	[111]
Martin Keown	1989 – 1993	120	[96]
Jack Jones	1933 – 1938	108	[98]
Duggie Livingstone	1921 – 1926	100	[95]

- Strangely, although Martin Keown failed to score whilst in an Everton shirt, during his time at the club he did score against Czechoslovakia for England in 1992 whilst with the Blues.
- Richard Dunne failed to score in 72 first team games for Everton, but scored twice for the Republic of Ireland during his Goodison career.
- The greatest number of games played without scoring for Everton, is the 277 appearances made by Brian Labone before his first goal for the club in October 1965. After a 2nd goal in February 1966, he ended his career with a further 229 appearances without a goal.
- Kevin Ratcliffe holds the record for the greatest number of games played at Goodison Park in a career without scoring. He made 235 home appearances between 1980 and 1991 without finding the net, the only goals in his career coming at Norwich in January 1983 and at Anfield in February 1986.
- Walter Balmer [brother of Robert] failed to score in his last 223 games for the club, scoring just one goal in 331 appearances in his career with the Blues. The Balmer brothers' combined career record for the club therefore amounted to just 1 goal in 519 matches.
- Kevin Ratcliffe matched Balmer's feat by also failing to score in his last 223 games for the club, after his single goal at Anfield in February 1986.

- After scoring his only goal for the club in the penultimate game of the 1928-29 season, Warney Cresswell played another 221 games for the Blues without scoring.
- Tommy Wright had 187 scoreless games before opening his Everton account against Southampton, at Goodison, in October 1968.
- The longest gap between a player scoring for Everton is 10 years and 23 days for David Johnson, between 30 September 1972 and 23 October 1982 – although for almost all of this period he was at other clubs.
- In terms of players who remained at the club, the record for the longest gap between goals is held by Ian Snodin. After scoring in the 5-0 win at Sheffield Wednesday, on 27 January 1988, his next goal was a single day short of 5 years later – at Wimbledon on 26 January 1993 – although he had been blighted by injury during that period.

Scoring substitutes

- Sandy Brown was the first Everton substitute to score for the club when he did so against Liverpool on 27 August 1966.
- The first substitute to score twice for the Blues was Stuart McCall, in the 1989 FA Cup Final. Stuart Barlow scored twice in a League match at Queens Park Rangers on 28 December 1992, after coming on as substitute.
- Adrian Heath scored a club record 7 goals as a substitute [from 26 appearances] between 1982 and 1988. Included in this tally were 4 from the bench in the 1985-86 season [2 League, 2 FA Cup].
- Prior to 'Inchy', the club record had been held by George Telfer, with 4 goals from the bench between 1974 and 1977.

HAT TRICKS

The complete list of Everton hat tricks

A McKinnon	v Derby County [h]	27 October 1888
Fred Geary	v Stoke City [h]	2 November 1889
Alex Latta	v Notts County [h]	7 December 1889
A Brady	v Derby County [h] [FA Cup]	18 January 1890
Fred Geary	v Derby County [h] [FA Cup]	18 January 1890
Alfred Milward	v Derby County [h] [FA Cup]	18 January 1890
T Wylie [4]	v Derby County [a]	13 December 1890
Edgar Chadwick	v Burnley [h]	27 December 1890
Alex Latta	v West Bromwich Albion [h]	7 November 1891
Alex Latta	v Notts County [h]	16 April 1892
Alex Latta [4]	v Newton Heath [a]	19 October 1892
Fred Geary	v Derby County [a]	5 November 1892
Alex Latta	v Derby County [a]	5 November 1892
Edgar Chadwick	v Sunderland [h]	30 September 1893
Jack Southworth [4]	v Sheffield Wednesday [h]	23 December 1893
Jack Southworth [6]	v West Bromwich Albion [h]	30 December 1893
Jack Southworth	v Small Heath [h]	3 September 1894
Jack Southworth	v Nottingham Forest [h]	15 September 1894
Alex Latta	v Small Heath [a]	3 November 1894
John Bell	v Southport [a] [FA Cup]	2 February 1895
John Bell	v Aston Villa [a]	30 September 1895
Edgar Chadwick	v Sheffield United [h]	5 October 1895
Alfred Milward	v Small Heath [a]	7 December 1895
T McInnes	v Stoke City [h]	14 December 1895
J Cameron	v Burnley [h]	28 November 1896
Jack Taylor	v West Bromwich Albion [a]	16 January 1897
John Bell	v West Bromwich Albion [h]	17 April 1897
A Hartley	v Wolverhampton Wanderers [h]	18 September 1897
Jimmy Settle	v Wolverhampton Wanderers [h]	7 September 1901
Jack Taylor	v Wolverhampton Wanderers [h]	7 September 1901
J Brearley	v Middlesbrough [h]	3 January 1903
Alex Young [4]	v Liverpool [h]	1 April 1904
Alex Young [4]	v Nottingham Forest [h]	5 November 1904
Jimmy Settle	v Southampton [h] [FA Cup]	3 March 1905
F Oliver	v Notts County [h]	14 October 1905
Jack Sharp	v Sheffield United [h]	10 February 1906
Alex Young [4]	v Manchester City [h]	3 September 1906

H Bolton	v Middlesbrough [h]	29 December 1906
H Bolton [4]	v Oldham Athletic [h] [FA Cup]	5 February 1908
Alex Young	v Manchester City [h]	26 September 1908
Bertie Freeman	v Sheffield United [a]	17 October 1908
Bertie Freeman	v Sunderland [h]	7 November 1908
Bertie Freeman	v Sheffield United [h]	20 February 1909
Bertie Freeman	v Chelsea [h]	20 March 1909
Bertie Freeman	v Sheffield Wednesday [a]	20 September 1909
Bertie Freeman	v Bolton Wanderers [h]	30 October 1909
Alex Young	v Blackburn Rovers [h]	19 November 1910
Bill Lacey	v Notts County [h]	21 January 1911
Tom Browell [4]	v Bury [h] [FA Cup]	8 February 1912
Tom Browell	v Southport [h] [FA Cup]	15 January 1913
Bobby Parker	v Manchester United [h]	26 December 1913
Joe Clennell	v Tottenham Hotspur [a]	2 September 1914
Bobby Parker	v Liverpool [a]	3 October 1914
Bobby Parker	v Sunderland [h]	21 November 1914
Bobby Parker [4]	v Sheffield Wednesday [a]	28 November 1914
Bobby Parker	v Manchester City [h]	12 December 1914
Bobby Parker	v Aston Villa [a]	10 February 1915
Bobby Parker	v Bolton Wanderers [h]	24 March 1915
Joe Clennell	v Bradford City [h]	8 November 1919
J Peacock	v Derby County [a]	11 September 1920
S Fazackerley	v Chelsea [h]	6 April 1921
S Davies	v Manchester United [h]	27 August 1921
R Irvine	v Aston Villa [h]	21 January 1921
Sam Chedgzoy	v Huddersfield Town [h]	14 April 1922
R Irvine	v Huddersfield Town [h]	14 April 1922
Wilf Chadwick	v Middlesbrough [a]	17 February 1923
Jack Cock	v Middlesbrough [h]	28 February 1923
Wilf Chadwick [4]	v Manchester City [h]	22 December 1923
Wilf Chadwick	v Tottenham Hotspur [h]	19 April 1924
Dixie Dean	v Burnley [a]	17 October 1925
Dixie Dean	v Leeds United [h]	24 October 1925
Dixie Dean	v Newcastle United [a]	12 December 1925
Dixie Dean	v Newcastle United [h]	24 April 1926
Dixie Dean [4]	v Sunderland [h]	25 December 1926
Dixie Dean [5]	v Manchester United [h]	8 October 1927
Dixie Dean	v Portsmouth [a]	29 November 1927

Dixie Dean	v Leicester City [h]	5 November 1927
Dixie Dean	v Aston Villa [a]	10 December 1927
Dixie Dean	v Liverpool [a]	25 February 1928
Dixie Dean [4]	v Burnley [a]	28 April 1928
Dixie Dean	v Arsenal [h]	5 May 1928
Dixie Dean	v Bolton Wanderers [a]	25 August 1928
Dixie Dean	v Portsmouth [h]	1 September 1928
Dixie Dean	v Newcastle United [h]	22 December 1928
Dixie Dean	v Bolton Wanderers [h]	29 December 1928
Dixie Dean	v Derby County [h]	1 January 1929
Dixie Dean	v Portsmouth [a]	28 September 1929
Tommy White	v Sunderland [h]	3 May 1930
Dixie Dean	v Stoke City [h]	22 November 1930
Dixie Dean [4]	v Oldham Athletic [h]	6 December 1930
Dixie Dean [4]	v Plymouth Argyle [h]	27 December 1930
Jimmy Stein [4]	v Plymouth Argyle [h]	27 December 1930
Dixie Dean [4]	v Crystal Palace [a] [FA Cup]	24 January 1931
Dixie Dean	v Charlton Athletic [a]	7 February 1931
Dixie Dean [4]	v Southport [h] [FA Cup]	28 February 1931
Jimmy Dunn	v Birmingham City [h]	29 August 1931
Tommy White	v Portsmouth [a]	2 September 1931
Dixie Dean	v Liverpool [a]	19 September 1931
Dixie Dean	v Sheffield United [a]	10 October 1931
Dixie Dean [5]	v Sheffield Wednesday [h]	17 October 1931
Dixie Dean [5]	v Chelsea [h]	14 November 1931
Dixie Dean	v Leicester City [h]	28 November 1931
Dixie Dean	v Blackburn Rovers [h]	26 December 1931
Dixie Dean	v Huddersfield Town [h]	19 March 1932
Dixie Dean	v West Ham United [h]	16 April 1932
Tom Johnson	v Blackburn Rovers [h]	27 December 1932
Dixie Dean	v Leicester City [h]	8 March 1933
Tommy White	v Blackburn Rovers [h]	14 October 1933
Dixie Dean	v Tottenham Hotspur [h]	29 December 1934
Albert Geldard	v Grimsby Town [h] [FA Cup]	12 January 1935
Jackie Coulter	v Sunderland [h] [FA Cup]	30 January 1935
Jimmy Cunliffe [4]	v Stoke City [h]	2 November 1935
Jimmy Cunliffe [4]	v West Brom [h]	11 April 1936
Dixie Dean	v Birmingham City [h]	25 April 1936
Dixie Dean	v West Bromwich Albion [h]	7 November 1936

Jimmy Cunliffe	v Derby County [h]	25 December 1936
Alex Stevenson	v Portsmouth [h]	30 April 1938
Robert Bell	v Leeds United [h]	22 October 1938
Tommy Lawton	v Middlesbrough [h]	5 November 1938
Tommy Lawton	v Doncaster Rovers [h] [FA Cup]	21 January 1939
Tommy Lawton [4]	v Middlesbrough [a]	11 March 1939
Stan Bentham	v Sunderland [h]	10 April 1939
Eddie Wainwright	v Sunderland [h]	15 February 1947
Jock Dodds	v Wolverhampton Wanderers [a]	21 February 1948
Jock Dodds	v Huddersfield Town [a]	28 April 1948
Jock Dodds	v Preston North End [h]	25 September 1948
Eddie Wainwright [4]	v Blackpool [h]	5 March 1949
Eddie Wainwright	v Huddersfield Town [h]	3 September 1949
Harry Catterick	v Fulham [a]	7 October 1950
John W Parker	v Hull City [h]	11 April 1952
Tommy Eglington [5]	v Doncaster Rovers [h]	27 September 1952
Harry Potts	v Bury [a]	13 December 1952
Dave Hickson	v Brentford [h]	7 February 1953
John W Parker	v Oldham Athletic [h]	29 August 1953
Dave Hickson	v Stoke City [a]	7 November 1953
Eddie Wainwright	v Derby County [a]	13 February 1954
John W Parker [4]	v Plymouth Argyle [h]	27 February 1954
John W Parker	v Rotherham United [h]	13 March 1954
Eddie Thomas [4]	v Preston North End [h]	8 March 1958
Jimmy Harris	v Tottenham Hotspur [a]	11 October 1958
Alex Shackleton	v Birmingham City [h]	14 November 1959
Eddie Thomas	v Nottingham Forest [h]	23 January 1960
Bobby Collins	v Newcastle United [h]	19 November 1960
Frank Wignall	v Tranmere Rovers [a] [League Cup]	21 December 1960
Bobby Collins	v Cardiff City [h]	15 April 1961
Roy Vernon	v Arsenal [h]	29 April 1961
Derek Temple	v Ipswich Town [h]	16 September 1961
Roy Vernon	v Cardiff City [h]	28 April 1962
Johnny Morrissey	v West Bromwich Albion [h]	29 September 1962
Roy Vernon	v Fulham [h]	11 May 1963
Fred Pickering	v Nottingham Forest [h]	14 March 1964
Fred Pickering	v Tottenham Hotspur [h]	29 August 1964
Alex Young	v Sheffield Wednesday [h]	31 August 1965
Johnny Morrissey	v Sunderland [h]	16 May 1967

Alan Ball [4]	v West Bromwich Albion [a]	16 March 1968
Alan Ball	v West Bromwich Albion [h]	28 September 1968
Joe Royle	v Leicester City [h]	30 November 1968
Joe Royle	v Southampton [h]	27 September 1969
Alan Ball	v Keflavik [h] [Euro Cup]	16 September 1970
Joe Royle [4]	v Southampton [h]	20 November 1971
David Johnson	v Southampton [h]	20 November 1971
Bob Latchford [4]	v Queens Park Rangers [a]	8 October 1977
Bob Latchford	v Coventry City [h]	26 November 1977
Bob Latchford [5]	v Wimbledon [h] [League Cup]	29 August 1978
Martin Dobson	v Wimbledon [h] [League Cup]	29 August 1978
Andy King	v Bristol City [h]	10 February 1979
Bob Latchford	v Leeds United [h]	13 November 1979
Bob Latchford	v Crystal Palace [h]	20 September 1980
Adrian Heath	v Notts County [h]	4 February 1984
Andy Gray	v Fortuna Sittard [h] [ECWC]	6 March 1985
Gary Lineker	v Birmingham City [h]	31 August 1985
Gary Lineker	v Manchester City [h]	11 February 1986
Gary Lineker	v Southampton [h]	3 May 1986
Paul Wilkinson	v Newport County [a] [League Cup]	7 October 1986
Wayne Clarke	v Newcastle United [h]	20 April 1987
Graeme Sharp [4]	v Southampton [a]	3 October 1987
Graeme Sharp	v Sheffield Wed [a] [FA Cup]	27 January 1988
Tony Cottee	v Newcastle United [h]	27 August 1988
Tony Cottee	v Wrexham [a] [League Cup]	25 September 1990
Graeme Sharp	v Wrexham [h] [League Cup]	9 October 1990
Peter Beardsley	v Coventry City [h]	21 September 1991
Tony Cottee	v Tottenham Hotspur [h]	5 October 1991
Tony Cottee	v Sheffield United [h]	21 August 1993
Paul Rideout	v Lincoln City [a] [League Cup]	21 September 1993
Tony Cottee	v Swindon Town [h]	15 January 1994
Andrei Kanchelskis	v Sheffield Wednesday [a]	27 April 1996
Gary Speed	v Southampton [h]	16 November 1996
Duncan Ferguson	v Bolton Wanderers [h]	28 December 1997
Kevin Campbell	v West Ham United [h]	8 May 1999
Nick Barmby	v West Ham United [a]	26 February 2000

● Kevin Sheedy scored 93 goals in his Everton career without notching up a hat trick. He scored 2 goals in a game on 9 occasions.

Most hat tricks

The following players have scored the most hat tricks for Everton during their careers, confirming the incredible domination by Dean of goalscoring records for the club.

	League	Cup	Total
Dixie Dean	34	2	36
Bobby Parker	7		7
Alex Latta	6		6
Bertie Freeman	6		6
Alex Young [1901 – 1911]	5		5
Bob Latchford	4	1	5
Tony Cottee	4	1	5
Jack Southworth	4		4
John W Parker	4		4
Edgar Chadwick	3		3
Wilf Chadwick	3		3
Tommy White	3		3
Nat Cunliffe	3		3
Eddie Wainwright	3		3
John Bell	2	1	3
Tommy Lawton	2	1	3
Jock Dodds	3		3
Roy Vernon	3		3
Alan Ball	2	1	3
Joe Royle	3		3
Gary Lineker	3		3
Graeme Sharp	1	2	3

Hat tricks scored on the opening day of the season

Joe Clennell	v	Tottenham Hotspur [a]	2 September 1914
Stan Davies	v	Manchester United [h]	27 August 1921
Dixie Dean	v	Bolton Wanderers [a]	25 August 1928
Jimmy Dunn	v	Birmingham City [h]	29 August 1931
Tony Cottee	v	Newcastle United [h]	27 August 1988

● After scoring a hat trick on the opening day of the season, prior to World War 1, Joe Clennell then scored hat tricks on the opening day of 3 of the 4 Lancashire League seasons during the War years. In the other season, he had to settle for 2 goals on the first day!

Highest number of hat tricks in a single season

Dixie Dean	8	1931-32
Dixie Dean	7	1927-28
Bobby Parker	6	1914-15
Dixie Dean	6	1930-31 [2 FA Cup]
Dixie Dean	5	1928-29
Bertie Freeman	4	1908-09

- The post-War record is 3 hat tricks in a season, jointly held by John W Parker in 1953-54 and Gary Lineker in 1985-86.

- The first League hat trick for the Blues was scored by A McKinnon, in what was the club's 8th League match against Derby County, in 1888-89.

- Tom Browell failed to score a hat trick in his 50 League games, but scored 2 in his 10 FA Cup matches for the club: against Bury in 1911-12 and Stockport the following year.

- Graeme Sharp is the only Everton player to score hat tricks in the 3 major domestic competitions, he also scored a hat trick against Newcastle United in the Full Members Cup in 1986-87. Strangely, 3 of these 4 hat tricks were scored before half-time.

- The best run of hat tricks is held by Dixie Dean, with 4 in 5 matches [the final 2 matches of the 1927-28 season and the first 3 games of 1928-29]. Later on in the 1928-29 season, he would also score 3 further hat tricks in 4 games. Bobby Parker scored 3 hat tricks in 4 matches in 1914-15.

- There are only 2 instances of players scoring hat tricks for Everton and losing. Jimmy Harris famously scored a hat trick when Everton lost 10-4 against Spurs at White Hart Lane, on 11 October 1958. However, he was not the first player with the club to achieve this unwanted feat, John Bell scored 3 times for the Blues at Aston Villa, on 30 September 1895, in a 4-3 defeat.

- Tommy Lawton achieved a rare feat against Middlesbrough, on 11 March 1939, by scoring 4 times in a game which Everton did not win, the sides drawing 4-4.

- The longest period, without any Everton player scoring a hat trick, occurred between the 8-0 win against Southampton, on 20 November 1971, and the match when Bob Latchford scored 4 times at Queens Park Rangers, on 8 October 1977. This run of almost 6 years stretched to 288 League and Cup matches.

- Kevin Campbell's hat trick against West Ham United in May 1999 meant that he became the first player to score hat tricks for three different clubs in the Premiership – having done so previously for Arsenal and Nottingham Forest.

Multiple hat tricks
Games in which 2 or more players scored a hat trick for Everton.

11-2 v Derby County [FA Cup] [h]	18 January 1890	A Brady, Fred Geary, Alfred Milward
6-1 v Derby County [a]	5 November 1892	Fred Geary, Alex Latta
6-1 v Wolves [h]	7 September 1901	Jimmy Settle, Jack Taylor
6-2 v Huddersfield [h]	14 April 1922	Sam Chedgzoy, Bobby Irvine
9-1 v Plymouth Argyle [h]	27 December 1930	Dixie Dean [4], Jimmy Stein [4]
8-0 v Southampton [h]	20 November 1971	Joe Royle [4], David Johnson
8-0 v Wimbledon [League Cup] [h]	29 August 1978	Bob Latchford [5], Martin Dobson

Hat trick doubles
These players scored hat tricks against the same club in both home and away fixtures in the same season.

Bertie Freeman	v Sheffield United	1908-09
Dixie Dean	v Newcastle United	1925-26
Dixie Dean	v Bolton Wanderers	1928-29
Tommy Lawton	v Middlesbrough	1938-39

- The greatest number of different players to score a hat trick in the same season for the Blues is 4, in the 1895-96 season [Chadwick, J Bell, Milward and McInnes]. The greatest number in the post-War era is 3, in the 1960-61 season [Vernon, Collins and Wignall] and 1978-79 [Latchford, Dobson and King].

- Duncan Ferguson's first hat trick for the club, against Bolton Wanderers, on 28 December 1997, was made up of 3 headed goals.

Hat trick victims

The following clubs have been on the receiving end of most hat tricks by Everton players.

Derby County	11	8 League, 3 FA Cup
West Bromwich Albion	9	9 League
Sunderland	9	8 League, 1 FA Cup
Southampton	7	6 League, 1 FA Cup
Sheffield Wednesday	7	6 League, 1 FA Cup

● Southampton have had a record 6 post-War hat tricks scored against them, all from the 1969-70 season onwards.

Most hat tricks in a decade

Decade by decade analysis of the number of League, Cup and European hat tricks scored by the club.

1888 – 1899	25		1950 – 1959	13
1900 – 1909	18		1960 – 1969	17
1910 – 1919	13		1970 – 1979	9
1920 – 1929	28		1980 – 1989	10
1930 – 1939	35		1990 – 1999	9
1940 – 1949	6			

League hat tricks against Everton

These players have scored League hat tricks against Everton since 1970.

John Richards	Wolverhampton Wanderers [a]	14 April 1973
David Cross	Coventry City [h]	16 August 1975
Ted McDougall	Norwich City [a]	6 September 1975
Alan Gowling	Newcastle United [a]	10 January 1976
Jim Melrose	Coventry City [a]	25 September 1982
Ian Rush	Liverpool [h]	6 November 1982
Gordon Davies	Chelsea [h]	22 December 1984
Jim Melrose	Charlton Athletic [a]	11 October 1986
Ian Wright	Arsenal [a]	21 December 1991
Darren Beckford	Norwich City [a]	21 March 1992
Andy Sinton	Queens Park Rangers [a]	28 December 1992
Les Ferdinand	Queens Park Rangers [h]	12 April 1993
Efan Ekoku	Norwich City [h]	25 September 1993
Bradley Allen	Queens Park Rangers [h]	20 November 1993
Chris Armstrong	Tottenham Hotspur [a]	26 December 1998
Ole Gunnar Solskjaer	Manchester United [a]	4 December 1999

Players who have scored 5 goals in a game against Everton

Tommy Johnson	for Manchester City [a]	15 September 1928
Derek Kevan	for West Bromwich Albion [a]	19 March 1960

- Tommy Johnson joined Everton in 1930.
- The last instance of a player scoring 4 goals in a game against Everton was Ole Gunnar Solskjaer, of Manchester United, at Old Trafford, on 4 December 1999.
- In the 1992-93 and 1993-94 seasons, 3 Queens Park Rangers players – Andy Sinton, Les Ferdinand and Bradley Allen – scored hat tricks in consecutive League games against the Blues.
- David Cross of Coventry, in 1975-76, provides the last instance of a player scoring a hat trick against Everton on the opening day of the season.
- Jim Melrose for Coventry [1982-83] and Charlton [1986-87] provide the only instance of players scoring a hat trick for different clubs in games against Everton.

EVERTON PLAYERS

350 or more appearances for Everton

Players who have made 350 or more appearances for Everton during their career in League, FA Cup, League Cup and European matches.

	Everton career	League	Others	Total
Neville Southall	1981 – 1997	578	148	726
Brian Labone	1958 – 1971	451	79	530
Dave Watson	1986 – 2000	423	105	528
Ted Sagar	1930 – 1952	463	32	495
Kevin Ratcliffe	1980 – 1991	359	113	472
Mike Lyons	1971 – 1982	389	71	460
Jack Taylor	1896 – 1910	400	56	456
Peter Farrell	1946 – 1957	422	31	453
Graeme Sharp	1980 – 1991	322	110	432
Dixie Dean	1925 – 1937	399	32	431
Tommy Eglington	1946 – 1957	394	34	428
TE Jones	1950 – 1961	383	28	411
Wally Fielding	1946 – 1958	380	30	410
Gordon West	1962 – 1973	335	64	399
John Hurst	1965 – 1976	347	52	399
Colin Harvey	1963 – 1974	320	64	384
Tommy Wright	1964 – 1973	308	63	371
Brian Harris	1955 – 1966	310	48	358

Players who have appeared in 300 or more League matches for Everton

		Total
Neville Southall	1981 – 1997	578
Ted Sagar	1930 – 1952	463
Brian Labone	1958 – 1971	451
Dave Watson	1986 – 2000	423
Peter Farrell	1946 – 1957	422
Jack Taylor	1896 – 1910	400
Dixie Dean	1925 – 1937	399
Tommy Eglington	1946 – 1957	394
Mike Lyons	1971 – 1982	389
TE Jones	1950 – 1961	383
Wally Fielding	1946 – 1958	380
Kevin Ratcliffe	1980 – 1091	359
John Hurst	1965 – 1976	347
Gordon West	1962 – 1973	335
Graeme Sharp	1980 – 1991	322
Colin Harvey	1963 – 1974	320
Brian Harris	1955 – 1966	310
Tommy Wright	1964 – 1973	308
Jack Sharp	1899 – 1910	300

3-decade men

These players have appeared in games for the club in 3 different decades.

Jack Taylor	1896 – 1910
Jack Sharp	1899 – 1910
Joe Donnachie	1906 – 1920
John Maconnachie	1907 – 1920
Ted Sagar	1930 – 1952
Brian Labone	1958 – 1971
Howard Kendall	1967 – 1982
Dave Watson	1986 – 2000

● Joe Donnachie achieved this feat despite playing in just 58 matches for the club. In 1919 he rejoined Everton, after leaving to join Oldham in 1908.

● Dave Watson is the only Everton player to appear for the club under 5 different managers: Howard Kendall [3 occasions], Colin Harvey, Mike Walker, Joe Royle and Walter Smith. During his time at the club he saw the management change on 6 occasions, as well as being caretaker manager himself at the end of the 1996-97 campaign.

Highest number of League appearances made, decade by decade

1888 – 1899	Edgar Chadwick	270
1900 – 1909	Jack Taylor	282
1910 – 1919	John Maconnachie	162
1920 – 1929	Hunter Hart	287
1930 – 1939	Ted Sagar	299
1940 – 1949	Ted Sagar	128
1950 – 1959	TE Jones	358
1960 – 1969	Brian Labone	402
1970 – 1979	Mick Lyons	310
1980 – 1989	Kevin Ratcliffe	303
1990 – 1999	Neville Southall	305

Consecutive appearances

These players have made 100 or more consecutive appearances for Everton in the 3 major domestic competitions and Europe.

266	Neville Southall	4 October 1987 – 9 January 1993
155	Cyril Lello	13 December 1952 – 10 March 1956
135	Jack Taylor	1 September 1896 – 24 March 1900
127	Joe Royle	18 May 1968 – 2 January 1971
120	George Wood	20 August 1977 – 14 November 1979
111	Dennis Stevens	14 March 1962 – 29 August 1964
108	Gordon West	18 May 1968 – 16 September 1970
106	Alec Troup	15 September 1926 – 25 December 1928
105	Neville Southall	17 December 1994 – 19 January 1997
103	Alfred Milward	30 March 1889 – 25 February 1893

● Neville Southall has uniquely made over 100 consecutive appearances on 2 occasions. Between 24 October 1987 and 25 January 1997, Southall missed just 5 out of the 466 games played by the club.

The 5 games Southall missed

v Wimbledon [h]	12 January 1993	Lost 1-2 [FA Cup]
v Aston Villa [a]	20 February 1993	Lost 1-2
v Oldham Athletic [h]	27 February 1993	Drew 2-2
v Lincoln City [a]	21 September 1993	Won 4-3 [League Cup]
v Aston Villa [a]	10 December 1994	Drew 0-0

● Jason Kearton was the Welsh international's replacement in all 5 games.

● Jack Taylor's 135 games were from the start of his Everton career.

● The next highest from debut is the 120 games of George Wood in the above list.

100 or more consecutive League appearances

212	Neville Southall	24 October 1987 – 10 February 1993
141	Cyril Lello	13 December 1952 – 10 March 1956
122	Jack Taylor	5 September 1896 – 24 March 1899
108	Joe Royle	21 May 1968 – 26 December 1970
100	Alec Troup	15 September 1926 – 25 December 1928

- Jack Taylor can uniquely claim to have made over 100 consecutive League appearances from his debut for the club.
- The post-War record is held by Dennis Stevens, who played in 99 consecutive League games after his debut on 14 March 1962.

Ever-presents

Fifty-five players have been ever-presents in a League season for the Blues. Neville Southall has achieved the feat on most occasions. The list of players who have achieved the feat on more than one occasion is:

7   Neville Southall

4   Jack Taylor

3   Edgar Chadwick, Arthur Milward, Richard Boyle, Gordon West, Brian Labone

2   Tom Booth, Ted Sagar, Peter Farrell, Cyril Lello, Dennis Stevens, Tommy Wright, John Hurst, Joe Royle, Mike Lyons, George Wood

- The last occasion a player was ever-present in a League season was Thomas Myhre in 1998-99.
- The last outfield player to be ever-present was Peter Beardsley in 1991-92.
- Edgar Chadwick [1888 – 1891] and Jack Taylor [1896 – 1899] were both ever-present in their first 3 seasons with the club.
- Only one post-War player has been ever-present in the League in his first 2 seasons with the club, goalkeeper George Wood, in 1977-78 and 1978-79.

Most appearances in a season

In the 3 major domestic competitions and Europe, the record for the highest number of appearances in a season is held by Neville Southall, who played in 62 competitive games in the 1984-85 season, when he was ever-present.

Players who have appeared in 57 or more games

62	Neville Southall	1984-85
60	Kevin Ratcliffe	1984-85
60	Trevor Steven	1984-85
58	Ken McNaught	1976-77
57	Kevin Ratcliffe	1983-84
57	Gary Stevens	1984-85
57	Derek Mountfield	1984-85

● Note that Southall, Ratcliffe, Steven, Stevens and Mountfield all played in the Charity Shield against Liverpool in 1984-85.

● The record number of appearances made in domestic games in one season was 58 matches, played by Ken McNaught, when he was ever-present in 1976-77.

● The first players to appear in 50 or more competitive games in a season for Everton were Brian Labone [52] and Fred Pickering [51], in 1964-65.

● The last Everton player to appear in 50 competitive games in a season was Neville Southall [51], in 1988-89.

Youngest post-War players

Age of the 10 youngest post-War Everton players on their debut.

16 years 282 days	Joe Royle	v	Blackpool [a]	15 January 1966
16 years 336 days	Francis Jeffers	v	Manchester United [a]	26 December 1997
17 years 40 days	Alan Tyrer	v	Fulham [a]	16 January 1960
17 years 47 days	George Sharples	v	WBA [h]	5 November 1960
17 years 51 days	Alec Farrall	v	Lincoln City [h]	22 April 1953
17 years 105 days	Roy Parnell	v	Wolves [a]	21 January 1961
17 years 107 days	Richard Dunne	v	Swindon [h] [FA Cup]	5 January 1997
17 years 123 days	Terry Darracott	v	Arsenal [h]	6 April 1968
17 years 127 days	Michael Branch	v	Manchester United [a]	21 February 1996
17 years 151 days	Jason Danskin	v	Luton Town [a]	28 May 1985

● Alec Farrall's 5 League appearances for Everton were all in different seasons, from 1952-53 to 1956-57.

Oldest post-War players

Age of the 10 oldest post-War players at their final appearance, up to the end of the 2000-01 season.

42 years 281 days	Ted Sagar	v	Plymouth [a]	15 November 1952
39 years 75 days	Neville Southall	v	Tottenham Hotspur [h]	29 November 1997
39 years 24 days	Richard Gough	v	Bradford City [h]	28 April 2001
38 years 319 days	Wally Fielding	v	Tottenham Hotspur [a]	11 October 1958
38 years 57 days	Dave Watson	v	Tottenham Hotspur [h]	15 January 2000
37 years 101 days	George Jackson	v	Portsmouth [h]	24 April 1948
36 years 348 days	Mark Hughes	v	Southampton [h]	14 October 2000
36 years 197 days	Cyril Lello	v	Aston Villa [h]	8 September 1956
36 years 74 days	Maurice Lindley	v	Blackburn Rovers [a]	16 February 1952
35 years 277 days	Wally Boyes	v	Blackpool [a]	9 October 1948

● The oldest pre-War player is believed to be Warney Cresswell, who was 40 years and 311 days when he made his final appearance for the club on 14 September 1935, at Bolton Wanderers.

● The oldest debutant in the club's history is Richard Gough, who was 37 years 126 days when he played against Manchester United, on the opening day of the 1999-00 season.

Youngest team

There are 2 contenders for the youngest side ever fielded by the Blues. Strangely, the games featured Johnny Morrissey, senior and junior, being the latter's only League appearance for the club.

v Leeds United [a] 16 April 1966

As the club faced an upcoming FA Cup Semi Final, Harry Catterick rested several players and, as a result, as well as a £2,000 fine from the FA, a side with an average age of 20 years 11 months faced the Yorkshire outfit: Rankin [aged 21], Brown [27], Darcy [19], Hurst [19], Smith [19], Glover [19], Husband [18], Humphreys [20], Royle [17], Trebilcock [21] and Morrissey senior [25].

v Luton Town [a] 28 May 1985

A combination of international calls and rested players after a long – and triumphant – season, resulted in this side averaging 22 years of age at Luton: Southall [26], Hughes [19], Bailey [28], Harper [24], Van Den Hauwe [24], Richardson [22], Morrissey junior [20], Wakenshaw [19], Wilkinson [20], Danskin [17], Walsh [17], plus substitute, N Rimmer [17].

Youngest players to reach milestones

The youngest players, in the post-War era, to reach the following milestones in League matches are:

100 League matches

| Joe Royle | v Nottingham Forest [h] | 1 November 1969 | 20 years 208 days |

200 League matches

| Joe Royle | v Leicester City [a] | 9 September 1972 | 23 years 155 days |

300 League matches

| Brian Labone v Sheffield United [h] | 14 January 1967 | 26 years 357 days |

400 League matches

| Peter Farrell | v Newcastle United [a] | 17 November 1956 | 34 years 94 days |

- John Hurst is the second youngest player to reach the landmark of 100 [21 years 249 days], 200 [24 years 22 days] and 300 League appearances [27 years 53 days].

- Both the youngest and oldest players ever to appear in League football played for Everton during the course of their careers: Albert Geldard was 15 years 158 days when he played for Bradford Park Avenue in 1929 and he would later play 167 League games for the Blues, as well as appearing in the 1933 FA Cup Final. Neil McBain was 52 years 120 days when he played for New Brighton in 1947. Earlier in his career he had made 97 League appearances for Everton, from 1923 – 1925.

Long playing career

These players enjoyed the longest playing career for the Blues.

22 years 302 days	Ted Sagar	18 January 1930 – 15 November 1952
16 years 44 days	Neville Southall	17 October 1981 – 29 November 1997
14 years 291 days	Howard Kendall	18 March 1967 – 2 January 1982
13 years 334 days	Joe Donnachie	17 February 1906 – 17 January 1920
13 years 196 days	Jack Taylor	5 September 1896 – 19 March 1910
13 years 149 days	Brian Labone	29 March 1958 – 24 August 1971
13 years 146 days	Dave Watson	23 August 1986 – 15 January 2000

- The longest gap between appearances for the club is 10 years 357 days, held by Joe Donnachie, between 7 September 1908 and 30 August 1919.
- The post-War record is held by David Johnson, who had 9 years 305 days between 28 October 1972 and 28 August 1982.

Briefest appearances

The following players have made just one substitute appearance as an Everton player, without ever starting a first team game.

Ian Bishop	v Manchester United [h]	5 May 1984
Darren Oldroyd	v Nottingham Forest [a]	11 May 1985
Neil Rimmer	v Luton Town [a]	28 May 1985
Phil Jones	v Southampton [h]	27 February 1988
Adam Farley	v Derby County [a]	7 February 1999
Peter Clarke	v Coventry [a]	20 January 2001

- Glen Keeley's Everton career lasted just 37 minutes before he was sent off in the Merseyside Derby on 6 November 1982; he was on loan from Blackburn at the time.

Unchanged teams

- The record for most consecutive games fielding an unchanged side, is 11 games, between 6 February 1954 and 10 April 1954, a run consisting of 10 League matches and a single FA Cup match.

- This run coincided with the record run of consecutive League matches with an unchanged side: 14 matches from 25 December 1953 to 10 April 1954. The only team change in a run of 17 League and Cup matches in this period was Eric Moore for Don Donovan, in a 4th Round FA Cup match against Swansea, on 30 January 1954.

- Everton reached the Semi Final of the FA Cup in 1909-10 by using an unchanged line-up for all 7 games in the competition, this was despite the fact that 14 other players featured in League matches during this period.

- The greatest number of unchanged games from the start of the season is 8 from the start of the 1938-39 season.

- The record for the greatest number of team changes is the 8 for the away game at Leeds United on 16 April 1966 – see above for youngest side.

Most and least players in a season

- The record for the greatest number of players in a League season is the 35 players used in the 1888-89 and 1919-20 seasons.

- The greatest number of players used in a League season in the post-War era is 34, in both 1997-98 and 1998-99 – the latter season saw 35 players used in all competitions.

- The least number of players used in a season is 18, in the 1968-69 season.

- In terms of League games, the fewest players used were the 16 in the victorious 1969-70 campaign, when 19 players were used in all competitions during the season.

Substitutes with 30 or more appearances

59 [including 6 Cup matches]	Danny Cadamarteri	1997 – 2001
57 [including 10 Cup matches]	Stuart Barlow	1991 – 1995
43 [including 10 Cup matches]	Sandy Brown	1963 – 1971
42 [including 13 Cup matches]	Alan Harper	1983 – 1993
35 [including 7 Cup matches]	Pat Nevin	1988 – 1992
33 [including 10 Cup matches]	Tony Cottee	1988 – 1994
32 [including 4 Cup matches]	Peter Beagrie	1989 – 1998

- The highest number of substitute appearances in a season is 21, by Stuart Barlow, in 1992-93.
- Everton's first ever substitute was John Hurst, in the League match at Stoke City, on 28 August 1965.
- The first time Everton used 2 substitutes in a match was at Newport County, in a League Cup game, on 7 October 1986 – Alan Harper and Neil Pointon.
- The first time Everton used 2 substitutes in a League game was at Queens Park Rangers on 2 September 1987 – Derek Mountfield and Kevin Sheedy.
- Three substitutes were used by the club for the first time at Queens Park Rangers, on 8 April 1996: Craig Short, Tony Grant and Michael Branch.
- The first Everton substitute to be substituted, was Stefan Rehn, against Millwall, on 14 October 1989. It was his last game for the club.
- The highest number of substitute appearances in a career, without a first-team start, was the 8 made by Warren Aspinall, between 1986 and 1987.

The name's the same

Four pairs of players with the same surname have played in the same side since the War.

Keith and Henry Newton	9 games	17 October 1970 – 23 October 1971
Bernie and Tommy Wright	3 games	4 March 1972 – 11 March 1972
Dave and Gary Jones	5 games	1 November 1975 – 20 March 1976
Mark and Stephen Hughes	19 games	15 March 2000 – 14 October 2000

- When Mark and Stephen Hughes scored against Watford on 1 April 2000, it was the first instance of 2 players with the same surname scoring for the club, in the same match, since Brian and Jimmy Harris scored at Nottingham Forest on 26 April 1958.
- For 3 matches in the 1955-56 season, 3 unrelated players with the same surname played for the club: Albert, Jimmy and Brian Harris.
- In total, Jimmy and Brian Harris played 138 matches together for the Blues, after both making their debut in the away game at Burnley, on 27 August 1955.

Fathers and sons

John Humphreys [1946 – 1950] and Gerry Humphreys [1966 – 1969]

Johnny Morrissey [1962 – 1972] and Johnny Morrissey [1984 – 1985]

Bill Kenny [1971 – 1974] and Bill Kenny [1992 – 1993]

Brothers

Bert Sharp [1899 – 1902] and Jack Sharp [1899 – 1910]

Robert Balmer [1903 – 1912] and Walter Balmer [1897 – 1908]

George Wilson [1906 – 1907] and David Wilson [1906 – 1907]

Andrew Browell [1912 – 1913] and Tom Browell [1912 – 1913]

- Andrew and Tom Browell, plus a 3rd brother, Gordon, all played together in the same Hull City side, one of only 9 such instances in League history.

Related players

Edgar Chadwick [1888 – 1899] and Arthur Chadwick [1889 – 92] [cousins]

George Saunders [1946 – 51] and Ron Saunders [1955] [cousins]

Tommy Wright [1964 – 73] and Billy Wright [1978 – 82] [uncle and nephew]

- In addition, Dennis Stevens [1962 – 65], was a cousin of the legendary Duncan Edwards.
- When Mike Walker was the manager of Everton, in the match against Tottenham on 26 March 1994, the opposition goalkeeper was his son, Ian.
- Billy Scott, the Everton keeper from 1904 and 1912, was the brother of Liverpool keeper, Elisha Scott.
- One other pair of brothers has played for Everton and Liverpool: Dave Watson and Alex Watson, the latter played 4 League games for the Reds.
- When Bob Latchford scored twice against Birmingham City, on 18 January 1975, the opposition keeper was his brother, Peter.

GOALKEEPERS

Most appearances

Goalkeepers with 100 or more League appearances for Everton.

		Appearances	Goals	Ratio
Neville Southall	1981 – 1997	578	682	1.18
Ted Sagar	1930 – 1952	463	763	1.65
Gordon West	1962 – 1973	335	361	1.08
Billy Scott	1904 – 1912	251	345	1.37
Tom Fern	1913 – 1924	219	295	1.35
Albert Dunlop	1956 – 1963	211	358	1.70
Jimmy O'Neill	1950 – 1960	201	308	1.53
Billy Muir	1897 – 1901	127	257	2.02
David Lawson	1972 – 1977	124	156	1.26
George Wood	1977 – 1980	103	108	1.05

- On the basis of goals per game conceded, George Wood is the most effective Everton keeper, conceding an average of 1.05 goals per game, followed by Gordon West [1.08] and Neville Southall [1.18]. It should be noted however that the number of goals per game has fallen over the years, when comparing the records of earlier keepers.

Stand-in keepers

- Sandy Brown took over from the injured Gordon West in the 4-2 win against Spurs at White Hart Lane on 7 March 1964.

- Brian Harris replaced the injured Andy Rankin in the 1-1 draw at home to Stoke City on 12 December 1964.

- After Gordon West was sent off in conceding a penalty at Newcastle on 28 October 1967, Sandy Brown took over the gloves, but unfortunately was unable to save Jim Iley's spot kick. The Blues lost 1-0.

- Mike Lyons took over goalkeeping duties at West Brom on 11 April 1973, when David Lawson was injured, although he was unable to prevent a 4-1 defeat. After this result it was announced that the club would be looking for a new manager, in succession to Harry Catterick.

- On 10 April 1982, against Manchester United, Lyons again took over in goal, when Neville Southall was taken off with concussion. The 3-3 draw was Lyons' last game in a blue shirt at Goodison and, in a career characterised by his versatility, it was fitting that he left the pitch wearing the number one jersey.

- After Neville Southall was sent off at Chelsea, on 12 October 1985, skipper Kevin Ratcliffe took over the gloves in a 1-2 defeat.

Substitute keepers

- When Neville Southall was sent off at Queens Park Rangers and Sheffield Wednesday in the 1992-93 season, substitute, Jason Kearton, came on as a replacement on both occasions. When Southall was suspended for the game against Aston Villa on 20 February 1993, Kearton's opposite number was Mark Bosnich, the first time in League history that both teams featured Australian keepers.

- In the final game of the 1992-93 season at Manchester City, when Jason Kearton came on as a substitute for Neville Southall, and Andy Dibble replaced Martyn Margetson in the City goal, it was the first time 4 goalkeepers had been used in a Football League game.

- Paul Gerrard made his debut for the Blues as a substitute for Neville Southall on 16 November 1996 at Goodison against Southampton.

- Steve Simonsen also made his Everton debut against Southampton, at the Dell as a substitute for Paul Gerrard on 22 January 2000.

- After Neville Southall was injured in the 1985-86 season, Pat Jennings was brought in as cover for Bobby Mimms, although he did not figure in a first team game. He remains the player with most international caps signed by the club.

Keeping nightmares

- Drew Brand's first game in goal for the club was a 2-5 defeat at Leeds United, on 29 November 1975. Not surprisingly, Brand had to wait 18 months for his second and final appearance for the club, a 2-0 win at Goodison against Newcastle on 24 May 1977.

- Although the Blues won the title in 1938-39, Harry Morton's only appearance of the season, as deputy for the ill Ted Sagar, was memorable for all the wrong reasons. Travelling to fellow title challengers, Wolves, Morton conceded 7 goals in a 0-7 defeat on 27 February 1939. 'Ted must have known something, getting out of this one,' Harry said – and how right he was.

- When playing for Norway, in the 2000 European Championships, Thomas Myhre became the first goalkeeper ever to be penalised for keeping the ball longer than the stipulated 6 seconds.

- Jimmy O'Neill's first appearance for the club was a 0-4 defeat at Middlesbrough, on 23 August 1950.

- C Menham's first game for the club was a 3-7 defeat at Sunderland, on 10 October 1925.

- Dai Davies had never been on the losing side in any of his 9 League matches for Swansea City before joining Everton in 1970, but he lost his first 2 for the Blues in March 1971.

- In what was Watford's first ever game in the English top-flight, against Everton, on 28 August 1982, Neville Southall carried a cross from Gerry Armstrong over the line, although the Irishman is credited with the goal.

Longest period between conceding goals

- Thomas Myhre is the only post-War Everton keeper to keep a clean sheet in his first 3 games for the club. The only other man to achieve this feat was J Caldwell in 1912.

- Bobby Mimms conceded one goal on his debut against Manchester City, on 26 October 1985, but had to wait nearly 11 hours [including 6 clean sheets] before next conceding a League goal, the longest period by any Everton keeper. Unfortunately, the goal in question – a last minute winner by Oxford United's Les Phillips, on 30 April – effectively cost the Blues the title in 1985-86. It was Mimms's only defeat in his first 17 League matches for the club.

Penalty saves

- In the Manchester United/Everton clash at Old Trafford on 2 March 1985, both keepers saved penalties, Gary Bailey from Kevin Sheedy and Neville Southall from Gordon Strachan.

- Centre-half Mark Wright's only appearance for the club, against Queens Park Rangers on 7 April 1990, would have been one to forget, had Neville Southall not saved a penalty conceded by the young defender in a 1-0 win for the Blues.

- Jim Arnold's only penalty save for the club was a last-minute stop in a 1-0 win at Norwich, on 22 January 1983.

- The most famous penalty save in the club's history is probably Andy Rankin's, in the European Cup 2nd Round tie against Borussia Moenchengladbach, at Goodison, on 4 November 1970. His save in the penalty shoot-out took the Blues into the next round.

Most goalkeepers

- The record for the greatest number of goalkeepers used by the Blues in a season is 6, set in 1892-93, when the season consisted of just 30 League games. The keepers concerned were Jardine [8 games], Murray [3 games], Pinnell [3 games], Rennie [4 games], Thomas [1 game] and Williams [11 games].

- Everton have fielded 3 keepers in a season on several occasions in the post-War era. The last occurrence was in 2000-01, when 3 keepers, Paul Gerrard, Steve Simonsen and Thomas Myhre, were used in the space of a week in games against West Ham and Charlton.

- Between 1 October and 19 October 1892, 4 keepers – Jardine, Pinnell, Thomas and Murray – kept goal in 4 consecutive League matches for the Blues. This remains a club record.

Oldest keeper

- Everton's oldest keeper, and also the oldest post-War player, is Ted Sagar, who was 42 years 281 days when he made his final appearance for the club at Plymouth, on 15 November 1952.

- Everton's oldest debutant goalkeeper in the post-War era, was Jim Arnold, who was 31 years 23 days when he made his debut against Birmingham City on 29 August 1981.

Youngest keeper

- The Blues' youngest post-War keeper is Jimmy O'Neill, who was 18 years 315 days on his debut against Middlesbrough in 1950.

INTERNATIONALS

Everton's internationals

- The most capped player in the club's history is Neville Southall, with 92 caps for Wales whilst with the Blues.

- The first Everton player to be capped internationally was John Holt when he was capped for England against Wales at Wrexham on 15 March 1890. Later that day, Fred Geary made his debut in a completely different England side and scored a hat trick in a 9-1 victory.

England international players

The most capped England internationals whilst with Everton.

Alan Ball	39
Ray Wilson	33
Brian Labone	26
Gary Stevens	26
Trevor Steven	25
Dixie Dean	16
Peter Reid	13
Bob Latchford	12
Tommy Wright	11
Gary Lineker	11

- Apart from some of those listed above, the most recent Everton players to be capped with England are: Nick Barmby, Paul Bracewell, Tony Cottee, Andy Hinchcliffe, Martin Keown, David Unsworth, Dave Watson and Michael Ball in 2000-01.

- The first player capped by England after the War, whilst with Everton, was Brian Labone, against Northern Ireland in Belfast, on 20 October 1962.

- The first time in the post-War era that as many as 4 Everton players appeared in the same England side, was when Gordon West, Tommy Wright, Brian Labone and Alan Ball all played away in Mexico on 1 June 1969.

- The only previous occurrence of 4 Everton players appearing in the same England side was in 1891 against Scotland, when John Holt, Fred Geary, Alfred Milward and Edgar Chadwick all played.

- The last England side to feature 4 Everton players was when Gary Stevens, Trevor Steven, Peter Reid and Dave Watson all appeared in the game against Switzerland on 28 May 1988.

- In the 1968 European Nations Cup 3rd place play-off, against Russia, 3 members of England's back 4 came from the club – Ray Wilson, Tommy Wright and Brian Labone.

- The last occasion on which 2 Everton players made their England debut in the same match was on 3 February 1971, when Joe Royle and Colin Harvey played against Malta.

- When Abel Xavier appeared for Portugal in the 2000 European Championship Semi Finals against France, he became the 4th Everton player to appear at that stage of the tournament. Ray Wilson, Brian Labone and Alan Ball all played against Yugoslavia in the 1968 Semi Final.

- Alan Ball and Michael Ball are the only players with the same surname capped by England while they were with Everton.

- When Nick Barmby played against France, in September 2000, he became the first player capped by England with Everton and Liverpool, and only the 2nd player after Bill Lacey, with Northern Ireland, to record such a feat.

Scotland international players

The most capped players with Scotland whilst with Everton.

David Weir	17
Graeme Sharp	12
Stuart McCall	11
Don Hutchison	10
Pat Nevin	8
Asa Hartford	7
Bruce Rioch	6
Bobby Collins	6
John Collins	5
Alex Scott	5
Torry Gillick	5

- Apart from some of those listed above, other recent cap winners have been Duncan Ferguson, Scot Gemmill, Andy Gray and Ian Wilson.

- The first Everton player to be capped with Scotland was John Bell, in 1896, against England.

- The last occasion when the Blues provided both forwards in an international line-up, was when Graeme Sharp and Andy Gray both played for Scotland, against Iceland, on 28 May 1985.

- The first time 3 Everton players appeared in the same Scotland side was in April 1999, against Germany, when Don Hutchison [who scored the winner], Scot Gemmill and David Weir all figured.

Wales international players

The most capped players with Wales whilst with Everton.

Neville Southall	92
Kevin Ratcliffe	58
Barry Horne	23
TG Jones	17
Dai Davies	16
Pat Van Den Hauwe	13
Roy Vernon	13
Gary Speed	9
Tom Griffiths	8

● Apart from those listed above, other recent cap winners have been Mark Pembridge, Dave Smallman and Mickey Thomas.

● The first Everton player to be capped with Wales was Joe Davies, against Scotland, in 1889.

● The first time 3 Everton players all appeared in the same Wales side occurred in April 1985, when Kevin Ratcliffe, Pat Van Den Hauwe and Neville Southall played against Spain.

Northern Ireland international players

The most capped players with Northern Ireland whilst with Everton.

Billy Scott	16
Alex Stevenson	14
Val Harris	14
Billy Cook	12
Billy Bingham	12
Dave Clements	12
Bryan Hamilton	11
Bobby Irvine	11
Bill Lacey	10

● Other cap winners since 1960 have been Norman Whiteside, Peter Scott and Tommy Jackson.

● The first Everton player to be capped by Northern Ireland was John Sheridan, when he played against Wales in 1903.

● After leaving Everton, Peter Scott had an interesting international career, going on to achieve the extremely rare feat of being the leading cap winner with 2 English League clubs simultaneously; not only that, but the 2 clubs concerned, Aldershot and York, were alphabetically first and last in the list of League clubs!

Republic of Ireland international players

The most capped Republic of Ireland internationals whilst with Everton.

Kevin Sheedy	41
Peter Farrell	26
Tommy Eglington	22
Jimmy O'Neill	17
Alex Stevenson	6
Richard Dunne	6
Don Donovan	5
Mick Meagan	4
Mick Walsh [1982]	4
Peter Corr	4

- Other recent cap winners with the Republic have been Jim McDonagh, Terry Phelan, Gerry Peyton, Gareth Farrelly, Eamonn O'Keefe and Mick Walsh [1978].

- The first Everton player to be capped by the Republic of Ireland was Tommy Eglington in 1947 against England.

- Tommy Eglington also won 7 caps for Northern Ireland, with Peter Farrell winning 6 caps.

- Gerry Peyton's 2 caps for the Republic, in 1992, make him the only player to be capped at the club without ever making a first team appearance.

International goalscorers

- Dixie Dean is Everton's leading goalscorer, with 18 goals in his 16 internationals.

- Everton's leading goalscorer for England in the post-War era is Gary Lineker, with 9 goals – including 6 in the 1986 World Cup Finals in Mexico.

- The last time a player scored for England whilst with Everton, was Martin Keown, against Czechoslovakia, on 25 March 1992.

- Edgar Chadwick's goal, after just 10 seconds, for England against Scotland at Ibrox, in 1892, is probably the quickest international goal by an England player.

Hat tricks for England whilst with Everton

These are the only England hat tricks scored by Everton players at international level.

Fred Geary	v Ireland [a]	March 15 1890
Dixie Dean	v Belgium [a]	11 May 1927
Dixie Dean	v Luxembourg [a]	21 May 1927
Fred Pickering	v USA [a]	27 May 1964
Gary Lineker	v Turkey [h]	16 October 1985

● Fred Pickering's hat trick was on his international debut and thus matched his 3 goals on his first Everton appearance earlier in the year.

Everton players who have scored in Wembley internationals

When Don Hutchison scored the winning goal for Scotland against England at Wembley in November 1999, it was only the 7th occasion an Everton player – and the first by an non-Englishman – had scored in over 200 Wembley internationals.

Fred Pickering	v Belgium	21 October 1964
Alan Ball	v USSR	6 December 1967
Joe Royle	v Yugoslavia	11 October 1972
Bob Latchford [2]	v Northern Ireland	7 February 1979
Trevor Steven	v Republic of Ireland	26 March 1985
Gary Lineker [3]	v Turkey	16 October 1985
Don Hutchison	v England	17 November 1999

Everton players who have scored against England

John Bell [Scotland]	at Hampden Park	4 April 1896
John Bell [Scotland]	at Hampden Park	7 April 1900
Bobby Irvine [Northern Irelandl]	at Anfield	20 October 1926
Alex Stevenson [Northern Ireland]	at Goodison Park	6 February 1935
Alex Stevenson [Northern Ireland]	at Belfast	23 October 1937
Peter Farrell [Republic of Ireland]	at Goodison Park	21 September 1949
Kevin Sheedy [Republic of Ireland]	at Cagliari	11 June 1990
Don Hutchison [Scotland]	at Wembley	17 November 1999

- Peter Farrell's goal for the Republic of Ireland at Goodison Park was considered to be the first occasion that a player in an international had scored an away goal on his home ground, and has been quoted as such in many publications. However, research for this book indicates that Alex Stevenson should, in fact, hold this honour.

Internationals at Goodison Park

- England have played 12 internationals at Goodison Park: winning 8 times, drawing on 3 occasions and losing once. Their defeat, against the Republic of Ireland in 1949 was memorable, being the first occasion they had lost to a country, outside the home countries, in England. Peter Farrell, of Everton, scored, and the winners also included future Blues Boss, Johnny Carey.

- Everton players to have scored at Goodison in full internationals for England are Harold Hardman [v Ireland in 1907] and Dixie Dean [v Ireland in 1928]. Alex Stevenson and Peter Farrell also scored for Northern Ireland and the Republic – see above.

- Ray Wilson, in the game against Poland in January 1966, was the last Everton player to play in a full international at Goodison. The game also featured Bobby Moore's only international goal in this country.

Everton players in the World Cup Finals

- In the 1970 Mexico Finals, 4 Everton players appeared in possibly England's finest ever side. Alan Ball, a winner in 1966 with Blackpool, was joined by Keith Newton, Brian Labone and Tommy Wright. All 4 appeared in the group match against Romania, when curiously one Blues full-back [Newton] was substituted for another Everton full-back [Wright].

- The 1986 side for the Mexico Finals also featured 4 Everton players – Gary Lineker, Peter Reid, Trevor Steven and Gary Stevens – who all played in the matches against Poland, Paraguay and Argentina.

- The first 5 post-War England international sides to feature 4 Everton players, all took place in Mexico – the international in 1969 against the host country, and the World Cup games in 1970 and 1986!

- 3 Scotland players have appeared in the World Cup Finals whilst with Everton – Alex Parker [1958], Graeme Sharp [1986] and Stuart McCall [1990].

- Kevin Sheedy made 5 appearances for the Republic of Ireland in 1990 when they reached the Quarter Finals – his goal against England making him the only other Everton player, apart from Gary Lineker, to score in the final stages.

- Ray Wilson [1966] and Slaven Bilic [1998 with Croatia] are the only Everton players who have played in a World Cup Semi Final.

- Anders Limpar played one game for Sweden in1994 in the USA.

Everton's overseas internationals

- Other Everton players to appear in internationals for overseas countries include Ibrahim Bakayoko [Ivory Coast], Marc Hottiger [Switzerland], Andrei Kanchelskis [Russia], Joe-Max Moore [USA] and Thomas Myhre [Norway].

- Robert Warzycha [Poland in 1993] and Daniel Amokachi [Nigeria in 1994], have both played for their countries in internationals at Wembley against England.

Everton's international managers

- After leaving Everton in 1977, Billy Bingham successfully guided Northern Ireland to the final stages of 2 World Cups, in 1982 and 1986.

- Former Blues mid-fielder, Bryan Hamilton, would also later manage Northern Ireland.

- Mark Hughes [Wales], in 2000, was not the first international player-manager to appear for Everton. Dave Clements was Northern Ireland player-manager in 1975, when he played for the Blues.

EVERTON MANAGERS

Everton managers

The comparative League records of all Everton managers, placed by using the number of points won as a percentage of those available, using 2 points for a win, is as follows

[note Howard Kendall's 3 spells in charge are shown separately]

		P	W	D	L	Points	%
Howard Kendall	1981 – 1987	252	131	59	62	321	64%
Harry Catterick	1961 – 1973	506	226	139	141	591	58%
Colin Harvey	1987 – 1990	126	51	37	38	139	55%
Gordon Lee	1977 – 1981	188	69	63	56	201	53%
Joe Royle	1994 – 1997	97	36	31	30	103	53%
Billy Bingham	1973 – 1977	146	53	48	45	154	52%
Johnny Carey	1958 – 1961	110	44	21	45	109	50%
Cliff Britton	1948 – 1956	316	110	90	116	310	49%
Howard Kendall	1990 – 1993	129	46	33	50	125	48%
Theo Kelly	1939 – 1948	93	35	17	41	87	47%
Walter Smith	1998 – 2001	114	34	33	47	101	44%
Howard Kendall	1997 – 1998	38	9	13	16	31	41%
Mike Walker	1994 –	31	6	9	16	21	34%

- Ian Buchan [1956 – 1958] has been excluded, as he did not have official status.

- Howard Kendall's spell between 1981 and 1987 was the most successful of any Blues' boss, netting the club 2 League titles, 1 FA Cup and 1 European Cup Winners' Cup. His combined League record as manager is: Played – 419, Won – 186, Drew – 105, Lost – 128, earning a total of 477 points. This means that Howard Kendall won 57% of the points available during his time as boss.

- Harry Catterick's spell included 2 League titles and 1 FA Cup victory and his 58% points won of the total available is superior to the 57% won by Howard Kendall over his 3 terms.

- It was fitting that Harry Catterick's final victory as Everton manager – a 1-0 win over Chelsea in April 1973 – should see Howard Kendall scoring the only goal.

Harry Catterick

In terms of League placings, Harry Catterick was the most successful manager of the 1960s, ahead of greats such as Sir Matt Busby, Bill Shankly, Bill Nicholson and Don Revie.

	1st	2nd	3rd	4th	5th	6th	Points
Harry Catterick	2	1	2	2	1	1	43
Don Revie	1	4	0	2	0	0	40
Matt Busby	2	2	0	1	0	0	35
Bill Shankly	2	1	1	0	2	0	34
Bill Nicholson	1	1	2	1	0	2	29

The points have been calculated using the Formula One system [1st = 10 points, 2nd = 6 points, 3rd = 4 points, 4th = 3 points, 5th = 2 points, 6th = 1point].

Harry Catterick's record in the 1960s

Champions	1962-63 and 1969-70
2nd	1960-61 [with Sheffield Wednesday]
3rd	1963-64 and 1968-69
4th	1961-62 and 1964-65
5th	1967-68
6th	1966-67

- His lowest League placing was 11th in 1965-66, when consolation was an FA Cup win.

- Brian Labone's 370 League appearances under Harry Catterick is the highest by any Everton player under one manager.

- Mike Lyons and David Johnson started their Everton careers under Harry Catterick and finished under Howard Kendall, making them the only players to appear for the 2 most successful managers in the club's history.

- When taking charge of Everton, against Sheffield Wednesday, in the 1966 FA Cup Final, he joined Herbert Chapman [Arsenal and Huddersfield 1930] as the only managers in Wembley history to manage a side in the Final, against a club they had previously been in charge of.

Howard Kendall

- Howard Kendall, in 1964, famously became the youngest player, at the time, to appear in an FA Cup Final at Wembley, being only 17 years and 345 days when playing for Preston against West Ham. However, an even more interesting scenario would have arisen if Manchester United had beaten West Ham in their Semi Final, for George Best was born on exactly the same day as Howard – 22 May 1946 – and consequently there would have been joint-record holders, had they both played in the Final.

- In winning the title, in 1985, he joined the select band of managers to have played in, and managed, the same club to title success.

- In his time as boss he signed 3 players who had been team-mates during his playing days: Jim Arnold [Blackburn Rovers], Adrian Heath [Stoke City] and David Johnson [Everton].

- Dave Watson and Neville Southall were the only players to appear for the club in each of his 3 spells in charge.

Other managers

- Colin Harvey's finish of 4th in his first season in charge in 1987-88, equalled Harry Catterick's record set for the best start by an Everton manager in 1961-62.

- Joe Royle had the longest unbeaten run at the start of any Everton manager's career: 5 games – including no goals conceded – until a 4-1 loss against Sheffield Wednesday, on 26 December 1994.

- Walter Smith played in the 1974 Scottish FA Cup Final for Dundee United, when they lost 3-0 to Celtic. His team-mates that day included Archie Knox and future Blues' legend, Andy Gray.

- The club with most managers, who have also managed Everton, is Blackburn Rovers with 3: Johnny Carey, Gordon Lee and Howard Kendall.

- Everton's 1968 FA Cup Final side featured 3 players – Howard Kendall, Colin Harvey and Joe Royle – who would later manage the club in the Final at Wembley. This is a unique feat in the competition's history.

Players who have played with and under Everton managers

The following players have appeared under an Everton manager, having previously played in the same Everton side as them: Stan Bentham, Wally Boyes and Ted Sagar [with Cliff Britton], TE Jones [with Harry Catterick], David Johnson and Mike Lyons [with Howard Kendall].

Everton players who had successful managerial careers at other clubs

Apart from Catterick and Kendall, 3 other Everton players have gone on to manage Championship-winning teams: Harry Potts [59 appearances from 1950 – 1956, won title with Burnley in 1960], Joe Mercer [170 appearances from 1934 – 1946, won title with Manchester City in 1968] and Ron Saunders [3 appearances in 1955, won title with Aston Villa in 1981].

TRANSFERS

Transfers

As a rule, clubs do not report exact transfer fees and the figures for these transactions are taken from the most widely accepted sources.

Purchases

Everton's most expensive transfer purchases since the War:

Aubrey Powell	£10,000	Leeds United	July 1948
Harry Potts	£20,000	Burnley	October 1950
Bobby Collins	£23,550	Celtic	September 1958
Roy Vernon	£27,000	Blackburn Rovers	February 1960
Jimmy Gabriel	£30,000	Dundee	March 1960
Alex Young	£40,000	Hearts	November 1960
Tony Kay	£55,000	Sheffield Wednesday	December 1962
Fred Pickering	£85,000	Blackburn Rovers	March 1964
Alan Ball	£110,000	Blackpool	August 1966
Henry Newton	£150,000	Nottingham Forest	October 1970
Joe Harper	£180,000	Aberdeen	December 1972
Bob Latchford	£350,000	Birmingham City	February 1974
Asa Hartford	£500,000	Nottingham Forest	August 1979
John Gidman	£650,000	Aston Villa	October 1979
Adrian Heath	£700,000	Stoke City	January 1982
Gary Lineker	£1,100,000	Leicester City	July 1985
Tony Cottee	£2,200,000	West Ham United	July 1988
Daniel Amokachi	£3,200,000	FC Bruges	August 1994
Duncan Ferguson	£4,000,000	Rangers	December 1994
Andrei Kanchelskis	£5,000,000	Manchester United	August 1995
Nick Barmby	£5,750,000	Middlesbrough	November 1996

- Although Nick Barmby remains Everton's most expensive single purchase, Duncan Ferguson could claim to be the most expensive player in the club's history, his £3.75 million transfer from Newcastle in 2000 means that his combined fees come to £7.75 million.

- Gordon West [£27,000] from Blackpool, in March 1962, and David Lawson [£80,000] in June 1972, were both record fees at the time for goalkeepers in British transfer history.

- The fee of £30,000 paid for full-back, John Barton, from Worcester City, in 1979, was a record fee for a non-League player at the time.

The 10 clubs from which Everton have made the most purchases

Blackburn Rovers	15
Burnley	10
Newcastle United	10
Preston North End	10
Aston Villa	9
Liverpool	9
Manchester United	9
Bolton Wanderers	8
Stoke City	8
Tranmere Rovers	8

- The purchase of striker Mick Ferguson from Coventry City, in 1981, remains the only occurrence of a player moving from the Sky Blues to Everton.

- Likewise, the transfer of Vinny Samways from Spurs, in 1994, was the first, and so far the only time a player has moved from White Hart Lane to Goodison Park.

- The purchase of Duncan McKenzie from Belgian club, Anderlecht, in December 1976, was the first time Everton had bought a player from a club outside the British Isles.

Sales

The largest progressive transfer sales since the War.

Tommy Lawton	£11,500	Chelsea	November 1945
Dave Hickson	£17,500	Aston Villa	September 1955
Jimmy Harris	£20,000	Birmingham City	December 1960
Bobby Collins	£30,000	Leeds United	March 1962
Roy Vernon	£40,000	Stoke City	March 1965
Fred Pickering	£50,000	Birmingham City	August 1967
Ernie Hunt	£65,000	Coventry City	March 1968
Alan Ball	£220,000	Arsenal	December 1971
Micky Walsh	£250,000	Queens Park Rangers	March 1979
Dave Jones	£250,000	Coventry City	June 1979
Dave Thomas	£325,000	Wolverhampton Wanderers	October 1979
John Gidman	£450,000	Manchester United	August 1981
Gary Lineker	£2,750,000	Barcelona	July 1986
Andrei Kanchelskis	£8,000,000	Fiorentina	January 1997
Francis Jeffers	£10,000,000	Arsenal	June 2001

- The 2 most recent instances of a player being both bought and sold in the same season are: Ernie Hunt, bought from Wolves and sold to Coventry City during the 1967-68 season and David Burrows, bought from West Ham United and sold to Coventry City during the 1994-95 season.

- The fee paid for Andrei Kanchelskis was a world record for a winger at the time.

Where Everton players went

The 10 most popular clubs to which players have moved from Everton.

Preston North End	24	Tranmere Rovers	14
Oldham Athletic	18	Blackburn Rovers	14
Liverpool	17	Burnley	13
Southampton	16	Manchester City	13
Birmingham City	15	Sunderland	12

Transfer fees

The following is an analysis of the transfer fees, both paid for and received, in 5 year cycles, starting from August 1970 to July 1975.

	Fees paid	Fees received
1970 – 1975	£1.7 million	£0.9 million
1975 – 1980	£3.9 million	£1.9 million
1980 – 1985	£4.5 million	£2.2 million
1985 – 1990	£9.3 million	£8.2 million
1990 – 1995	£24.0 million	£9.6 million
1995 – 2000	£63.1 million	£55.5 million

- The list shows how fees have rocketed in the past 10 years, and especially since 1995. In fact, the club's expenditure in the summer of 2000 [around £19 million] equates to the total amount paid by Everton in the 20 years up to 1990!

Mersey moves

- The following players have moved from Liverpool to Everton during their careers: Gary Ablett, Peter Beardsley, Dick Forshaw, Alan Harper, David Johnson, Johnny Morrissey, Jimmy Payne, Kevin Sheedy and Harold Uren.

- The following players have moved from Everton to Liverpool: Nick Barmby, Arthur Berry, Fred Geary, Patrick Gordon, Tom Gracie, Bill Hartill, Abraham Hartley, Dave Hickson, Tommy Johnson, Bill Lacey, Alex Latta, Duncan McLean, Tony McNamara, Frank Mitchell, David Murray, Donald Sloan and T Wyle.

- Other players to have also played for both clubs during their career include: Don Hutchison, David Johnson, Neil McBain and Steve McMahon.

- The most expensive move from Liverpool to the Blues is the £1 million paid for Peter Beardsley in 1991. The biggest fee in the opposite direction is £6 million in 2000 for Nick Barmby.

- Peter Beardsley also had brief spells at both Manchester United and Manchester City, making him the only player to appear for the 4 clubs from Liverpool and Manchester.

Back home

Players who have had 2 spells in their Everton career.

John Bell	1892 – 1898 and 1901 – 1903
Joe Donnachie	1906 – 1908 and 1919 – 1920
Duncan Ferguson	1994 – 1998 and 2000 –
Alan Harper	1983 – 1988 and 1991 – 1993
Dave Hickson	1948 – 1955 and 1957 – 1959
Andy King	1976 – 1980 and 1982 – 1984
David Johnson	1970 – 1972 and 1982 – 1984
Bob Kelso	1888 – 1889 and 1891 – 1995
Howard Kendall	1967 – 1974 and 1981 – 1982 [player/manager]
David Unsworth	1992 – 1997 and 1998 –

- In addition, Terry Curran, Brett Angell and Peter Beagrie all had 2 spells as players, each having one spell on loan and one following a permanent transfer.

- Alan Harper is the only player in the club's history to have been purchased twice by the same manager, being bought by Howard Kendall in 1983 and 1991. He was also bought by the Everton Manager of the Millennium whilst at Manchester City.

Transferred back

Players transferred back to the clubs from where they were purchased since 1970.

Bernie Wright	Walsall	1972 – 1973
David Smallman	Wrexham	1975 – 1980
Martin Dobson	Burnley	1974 – 1979
Bruce Rioch	Derby County	1976 – 1977
Jim McDonagh	Bolton	1980 – 1981
Paul Bracewell	Sunderland	1984 – 1989
Mick Milligan	Oldham Athletic	1990 – 1991
Tony Cottee	West Ham United	1988 – 1994
John Hills	Blackpool	1996 – 1997
Marco Materazzi	Perugia	1998 – 1999

[years shown are the time at Everton]

ATTENDANCES

Average crowds

Everton have been watched in League home matches, since the beginning of the Football League, in 1888, by just over 60 million spectators, the 3rd highest total for any League club after Liverpool and Manchester United. In 1981 the Blues were the first side to be watched at home by 50 million spectators. The average home attendances for the following 10 year cycles [12 years from 1888] over that period are.

1888 – 1899	13,501
1900 – 1909	17,998
1910 – 1919	21,750
1920 – 1929	31,276
1930 – 1939	33,229
1940 – 1949	43,532
1950 – 1959	40,079
1960 – 1969	45,152
1970 – 1979	34,901
1980 – 1989	26,936
1990 – 1999	30,086

- The average home attendance for all home League games is 30,581.

- The highest average attendance is 51,603 for the Championship-winning season of 1962-63. This is the only occasion on which the magic 50,000 barrier has been broken. In contrast, Everton had an average of just over 7,000 for their first season of League football in 1888-89.

- The Blues' record, of having the highest average attendance in 13 seasons, is only exceeded by Manchester United. The last time this was achieved was in 1962-63.

- Everton averaged 44,493 in their final season in the 2nd Division in 1953-54, one of the highest ever average attendances recorded outside the English top-flight. A crowd of 62,865 saw the game against Birmingham City on 24 April 1954, one of the biggest gates in Division 2 history.

- In recent times, the figure for the 1983-84 season, of 19,343, is the only occasion on which the average has fallen below 20,000 since the Championship-winning year of 1914-15.

Home attendances – highs

Home League crowds over 70,000 [all at Goodison Park].

78,299	v Liverpool	18 September 1948
76,839	v Preston North End	28 August 1954
75,322	v Wolverhampton Wanderers	27 December 1954
74,867	v Burnley	27 December 1960
72,488	v Liverpool	22 September 1962
72,007	v Manchester United	4 September 1957
71,150	v Liverpool	16 September 1950
71,008	v Blackpool	7 April 1950
70,812	v Liverpool	27 August 1949

- The above attendance against Liverpool, in 1962, was the last occasion that a League fixture attracted a crowd of over 70,000 in this country.

- Prior to the War, the highest League crowd at home had been the 65,729 for the Merseyside Derby, on 15 October 1927.

- In addition to the above, 77,920 watched the FA Cup 5th Round clash against Manchester United, at Goodison, on 14 February 1953. However, a crowd of 104,487 [64,318 at the ground and 40,169 on closed circuit TV at Anfield], witnessed the 5th Round tie at Goodison, between Everton and Liverpool, on 11 March 1967.

- The highest gate for any mid-week League match in this country is the 72,077 for the home match against Manchester United on 4 September 1957.

- The last time a home League crowd exceeded 60,000 was when 63,938 saw the Merseyside Derby, on 27 August 1968. The last home League attendance in excess of 50,000 was the crowd of 51,509, for the same fixture, on 21 September 1985.

- The game when Everton clinched the title against Queens Park Rangers, on 6 May 1985, is the only crowd of over 50,000 for a home League game, other than for a derby, since 52,000 for the match against Manchester United in August 1972.

- The highest attendance for a European match at Goodison was the 62,408 who saw the 1st leg of the European Cup 1st Round tie against Inter Milan, on 18 September 1963.

- The highest attendance for a home League Cup tie was on 21 January 1987, when 53,323 saw the Quarter Final match against Liverpool.

- The highest attendance for a Premiership game at Goodison was the 40,260 who saw the game against Liverpool on 16 April 2001.

Home attendances – lows

- The lowest ever attendance for an Everton home game was when 2,079 people saw Everton against West Bromwich Albion, in the first season of League football in 1888-89.

- In the post-War period, the lowest League attendance at Goodison was when 10,829 saw the Division 2 match against Fulham, on 25 March 1953. The last attendance of under 10,000 for a League game at Goodison was 8,199 against Leicester, on 8 March 1939.

- The lowest home gate in any of the 3 major domestic competitions at Goodison was 7,514 against Wrexham, in the 2nd Round of the League Cup, on 9 October 1990. The lowest against top-flight opposition was 9,080 against Coventry City in the next round, on 9 November 1983.

- In the top division, the lowest post-War gate was 12,972 for the 1-0 win over Coventry City on 2 May 1983.

- The lowest Premiership attendance at Goodison was 13,265, for the match against Southampton, on 4 December 1993. It was after this game that Howard Kendall resigned as manager.

- The lowest post-War gate for an FA Cup tie is believed to be the 15,293 for the 3rd Round replay against Wimbledon, on 12 January 1993.

- The smallest gate for a European match at Goodison was 16,277 against UC Dublin, in the Cup Winners' Cup 1st Round, on 2 October 1984.

Away attendances – highs

Crowds in excess of 60,000 in away League games.

67,528	v	Manchester United	3 February 2001
65,334	v	Arsenal	31 August 1954
64,555	v	Arsenal	10 September 1938
63,675	v	Manchester United	29 August 1962
63,206	v	Manchester United	31 August 1963
61,879	v	Manchester United	17 April 1976
61,663	v	Aston Villa	24 October 1931
61,311	v	Manchester United	10 August 1968
61,114	v	Manchester United	31 August 1966

- The last crowd of over 60,000 for an away tie in the FA Cup, was at Old Trafford for the Quarter Final, on 1 March 1969, when 63,464 saw the game.
- The highest crowd to watch any Everton away game was the 78,000 at the Olympic Stadium for the Cup Winners' Cup Semi Final, against Bayern Munich, on 10 April 1985.
- The highest attendances for a League Cup tie is 57,738, who saw Everton at Old Trafford v Manchester United on 1 December 1976.

Away attendances – lows

- The lowest post-War attendance for an Everton away game in the League was 3,039 for the match at Wimbledon on 26 January 1993. This is the lowest top-division attendance since the War.

EVERTON
IN 2000-01 SEASON

Everton 2000-01

This chapter looks at Everton in the 2000-01 season, a disappointing campaign which saw the Blues finish 16th in the Premiership and suffer early exits in the FA Cup and [yet again] in the Worthington Cup.

What follows is a summary of the 42 League and Cup games played in the season, showing line-ups and attendances etc.

For the majority of the games, a brief description of what happened is provided. In keeping with the rest of the book, the comments have a statistical focus, and some relevant extra information has been provided to place some of the achievements in an historical context.

FA Premier League

Saturday 19 August 2000 • Elland Road • Attendance 40,010
Kick-off 3pm • Referee DJ Gallagher [Banbury]

Leeds United 2   Everton 0
Smith 16, 37

The teams

Paul Gerrard, Steve Watson*, David Weir, David Unsworth, Alessandro Pistone, Scot
Gemmill [Paul Gascoigne], Alex Nyarko*, Stephen Hughes [Duncan Ferguson], Michael
Ball, Francis Jeffers*, Mark Hughes [Joe Max Moore].

Nigel Martyn, Gary Kelly, Lucas Radebe, Ian Harte, Eirik Bakke [Danny Mills], Olivier
Dacourt, Lee Bowyer, Alan Smith, Mark Viduka, Michael Bridges [Darren Huckerby],
Jonathan Woodgate.

*booked **sent off

● Alan Smith scored the first 2 goals of the Premiership season against the Blues, now
  without a win at Elland Road in the League since September 1951.

FA Premier League
Wednesday 23 August 2000 • Goodison Park • Attendance 36,300
Kick-off 7.45pm • Referee NS Barry [Scunthorpe]

Everton 3   Charlton Athletic 0
Jeffers 54
Ferguson 84, 90

The teams

Paul Gerrard, Steve Watson, Alessandro Pistone [David Unsworth], Richard Gough, David Weir, Alex Nyarko, Stephen Hughes, Francis Jeffers*, Thomas Gravesen, Paul Gascoigne [Joe Max Moore], Mark Hughes* [Duncan Ferguson].

Dean Kiely, Radostin Kishishev, Chris Powell, Graham Stuart, Richard Rufus*, Carl Tiler**, Mark Kinsella, Andy Hunt, John Robinson [Scott Parker], Claus Jensen [Shaun Newton], Kevin Lisbie [Steve Brown].

*booked **sent off

- Ferguson's first appearance, following his return to the club, sees him create Everton history, as the first substitute to score twice in a League game at Goodison.

- Former Blue, Carl Tiler, was sent off for Charlton in the first half.

Players scoring 2 goals after coming on as substitute

Stuart McCall	v Liverpool [n] [FA Cup]	20 May 1989
Tony Cottee	v Liverpool [h] [FA Cup]	20 February 1991
Stuart Barlow	v Queens Park Rangers [a]	28 December 1992
Daniel Amokachi	v Tottenham Hotspur [n] [FA Cup]	9 April 1995
Nick Barmby	v Scunthorpe [h] [League Cup]	1 October 1997
Duncan Ferguson	v Charlton Athletic [h]	23 August 2000

FA Premier League
Saturday 26 August 2000 • Goodison Park • Attendance 34,840
Kick-off 3pm • Referee MA Riley [Leeds]

Everton 2
Jeffers 28
Gravesen 40

Derby County 2
Sturridge 52
Strupar 68

The teams
Paul Gerrard, Steve Watson, Richard Gough [Paul Gascoigne], David Weir, David Unsworth, Niclas Alexandersson, Alex Nyarko, Stephen Hughes, Francis Jeffers [Mark Hughes], Thomas Gravesen, Joe Max Moore* [Danny Cadamarteri].

Mart Poom, Deon Burton, Danny Higginbottom [Stefan Schnoor], Richard Jackson [Dean Sturridge], Steve Elliott, Stefano Eranio [Chris Riggott], Bjorn Otto Bragstad, Branko Strupar, Simo Valakari, Adam Murray, Seth Johnson.

*booked **sent off

● Everton throw away 2 points, after squandering a 2-0 half-time lead.

FA Premier League

Tuesday 5 September 2000 • White Hart Lane • Attendance 35,316
Kick-off 7.45pm • Referee B Knight [Orpington]

Tottenham Hotspur 3

Rebrov 45, 61 [pen]
Ferdinand 62

Everton 2

Jeffers 23
Nyarko 41

The teams

Paul Gerrard, Steve Watson, David Weir, David Unsworth*, Niclas Alexandersson*, Alex Nyarko, Stephen Hughes [Alec Cleland], Francis Jeffers, Thomas Gravesen, Paul Gascoigne [Danny Cadamarteri], Mark Hughes [Joe Max Moore].

Neil Sullivan, Stephen Carr, Steffen Freund, Sol Campbell, Chris Perry, Darren Anderton [Stephen Clemence], Tim Sherwood, Les Ferdinand [Steffen Iversen] Sergei Rebrov* Oyvind Leonhardsen, Ben Thatcher [Mauricio Taricco].

*booked **sent off

- Les Ferdinand scores his 13th League goal against Everton, the most by any current Premiership player.

- Again, Everton squander a 2-goal lead and lose an away match, in the League, for the first time since the 3-2 loss at Anfield on 21 November 1970.

- Everton have now lost 4 games in the Premiership at White Hart Lane after leading during the match.

FA Premier League

Saturday 9 September 2000 • The Riverside • Attendance 30,885
Kick-off 3pm • Referee SG Bennet [Orpington]

Middlesbrough 1
Watson [og] 7

Everton 2
Jeffers 54, 87

The teams

Paul Gerrard, Steve Watson, David Weir, Niclas Alexandersson, Alex Nyarko [Alec Cleland], Stephen Hughes, Francis Jeffers, Thomas Gravesen, Paul Gascoigne, Mark Hughes [Kevin Campbell], Abel Xavier.

Mark Schwarzer, Curtis Fleming*, Dean Gordon, Steve Vickers [Jason Gavin], Gialuca Festa, Christian Karembeu, Paul Ince [Brian Deane], Alen Boksic, Joseph-Desire Job [Hamilton Ricard], Phil Stamp*, Noel Whelan *.

*booked **sent off

● Jeffers scores twice in a game for the first time in his Everton career. He becomes the first player since Fred Pickering, in the 1965-66 season, to score 5 goals in the first 5 games of the season.

Best-scoring start to top-flight season [first 5 games] since Dixie Dean

Tommy Lawton	7 goals	1938-39
Eddie Wainwright	5 goals	1949-50
Fred Pickering	5 goals	1965-66
Francis Jeffers	5 goals	2000-01

FA Premier League
Saturday 16 September 2000 • Goodison Park • Attendance 38,541
Kick-off 3pm • Referee DJ Gallagher [Banbury]

Everton 1
Gravesen 54

Manchester United 3
Butt 27
Giggs 29
Solskjaer 38

Teams
Paul Gerrard, Richard Dunne*, David Weir, Steve Watson, Stephen Hughes [David Unsworth], Niclas Alexandersson, Thomas Gravesen, Alex Nyarko*, Paul Gascoigne [Scot Gemmill*], Francis Jeffers*, Mark Hughes [Kevin Campbell].

Fabien Barthez [Ramond Van Der Gouw], Denis Irwin, Gary Neville, Wes Brown, Mikael Silvestre, David Beckham, Paul Scholes [Phil Neville], Nicky Butt, Ryan Giggs [Dwight Yorke], Ole Gunnar Solskjaer, Teddy Sheringham.
*booked **sent off

● United's win means that they have won 5 and drawn 1 of their last 6 Premiership visits to Goodison Park.

Worthington Cup 2nd Round, 1st leg
Wednesday 20 September 2000 • Goodison Park • Attendance 25,564
Kick-off 8pm • Referee SJ Baines [Chesterfield]

Everton 1
Campbell 50

Bristol Rovers 1
Hogg 87

The teams
Paul Gerrard, Steve Watson, Alessandro Pistone [Stephen Hughes*], David Weir, David Unsworth, Niclas Alexandersson [Joe Max Moore], Alex Nyarko, Kevin Campbell, Michael Ball [Paul Gascoigne], Francis Jeffers, Alec Cleland.

Nick Culkin, Steve Foster, Vitalis Astafijeus, Mickey Evans [Mark Walters], Marcus Andreasson [Dwayne Plummer], Nathan Ellington [Clinton Ellis], Simon Bryant, Marcus Bignot, Lewis Hogg, Che Wilson, Scott Jones.
*booked **sent off

FA Premier League
Sunday 24 September 2000 • Filbert Street • Attendance 18,084
Kick-off 4pm • Referee AG Wiley [Burntwood]

Leicester City 1   **Everton 1**
Akinbiyi 23   Unsworth 52

The teams
Paul Gerrard, Richard Dunne, Steve Watson*, David Weir, Niclas Alexandersson, Paul
Gascoigne, Thomas Gravesen, Alex Nyarko, David Unsworth, Francis Jeffers [Joe Max
Moore], Kevin Campbell [Mark Hughes].

Tim Flowers, Gary Rowett, Matt Elliott, Gerry Taggart*, Steve Guppy, Andrew Impey
[Stan Collymore], Neil Lennon, Muzzy Izzet, Robbie Savage*, Darren Eadie [Phil
Gilchrist], Ade Akinbiyi [Richard Cresswell].
*booked **sent off

● Everton's draw, in their first live TV outing of the season, sees them deprive Leicester of
the chance of going top of the table for the first time since 1963.

Worthington Cup 2nd Round, 2nd leg
Wednesday 27 September 2000 • The Memorial Stadium • Attendance 11,046
Kick-off 7.45pm • Referee PA Durkin [Portland]

Bristol Rovers 1   **Everton 1**
Bignot 58   Jeffers 14

The teams
Paul Gerrard, Richard Dunne, Steve Watson, David Unsworth [Michael Ball], Niclas
Alexandersson, Thomas Gravesen*, Joe Max Moore, Alex Nyarko, Stephen Hughes*,
Mark Hughes* [Kevin Campbell], Francis Jeffers [Alec Cleland].

Nick Culkin, Marcus Andreasson [Mark Walters], Steve Foster, Scott Jones, Che Wilson,
Lewis Hogg [Dwayne Plummer], Marcus Bignot, Simon Bryant [Michael Meaker], Vitalis
Astafjeus, Clinton Ellis, Nathan Ellington.
*booked **sent off

● A 4-2 defeat on penalties means that Everton's appalling record in this competition
continues.

Penalty shoot-outs in major competitions
v Borussia Moenchengladbach [h] [Euro Cup]   Won 4-3   4 November 1970
v Sunderland [h] [League Cup]   Lost 5-6   11 November 1998
v Bristol Rovers [a] [League Cup]   Lost 2-4   27 September 2000

FA Premier League

Saturday 30 September 2000 • Goodison Park • Attendance 32,59
Kick-off 3pm • Referee JT Winter [Stockton-on-Tees]

Everton 0

Ipswich Town 3
McGreal 19
Stewart 49, 60

The teams

Paul Gerrard, Steve Watson, David Weir, David Unsworth [Stephen Hughes], Niclas Alexandersson [Kevin McLeod], Alex Nyarko*, Thomas Gravesen, Paul Gascoigne, Scot Gemmill, Kevin Campbell, Joe Max Moore [Mark Hughes].

Richard Wright, Fabian Wilnis, Jamie Clapham, John McGreal, Jim Magilton, Matt Holland, Marcus Stewart [David Johnson], Richard Naylor [James Scowcroft], Jermaine Wright, Titus Bramble, Hermann Hreidarsson.
*booked **sent off

● Everton concede 3 goals at home, in consecutive Premiership games, for the first time since 1995.

FA Premier League

Saturday 14 October 2000 • Goodison Park • Attendance 29,491
Kick-off 3pm • Referee DR Elleray [Harrow-on-the-Hill]

Everton 1
Ball [pen] 81

Southampton 1
Dodd 76

The teams

Paul Gerrard, Steve Watson, David Weir, Alex Nyarko, Kevin Campbell, Mark Pembridge [Stephen Hughes], Michael Ball, Thomas Gravesen, Paul Gascoigne*, Mark Hughes [Joe Max Moore], Richard Dunne.

Paul Jones, Jason Dodd, Chris Marsden* Claus Lundekvam, Matthew Oakley, Kevin Davies*, Marian Pahars, Wayne Bridge, Tahar El Khalej, Hassan Kachloul* Trond Soltvedt.
*booked **sent off

● The first sub-30,000 gate for a Premiership match at Goodison since Wimbledon in December 1997 and only the second in 6 years.

FA Premier League

Saturday 21 October 2000 • St James Park • Attendance 51,625
Kick-off 3pm • Referee MR Halsey [Welwyn Garden City]

Newcastle United 0

Everton 1
Campbell 80

The teams

Paul Gerrard, Steve Watson, David Weir, Alex Nyarko, Kevin Campbell, Mark Pembridge* [Gary Naysmith], Michael Ball*, Thomas Gravesen*, Paul Gascoigne, Abel Xavier, Idan Tal [David Unsworth].

Shay Given, Warren Barton [Kevin Gallagher], Didier Domi, Alain Goma, Robert Lee, Kieron Dyer, Alan Shearer, Gary Speed, Nolberto Solano, Daniel Cordone [Lomona Tresor Lua Lua], Aaron Hughes.

*booked **sent off

- Campbell makes it 4 goals in 3 visits to St James' Park in a blue shirt.
- Idan Tal becomes the first Everton player for 37 years [since Tony Kay] to have only 3 letters in his surname.
- The first time in 10 away games in the Premiership that the Blues have kept a clean sheet.

FA Premier League

29 October 2000 • Anfield • Attendance 44,718
Kick-off • Referee • PA Durkin [Portland]

Liverpool 3	Everton 1
Barmby 12	Campbell 17
Heskey 56	
Berger [pen] 78	

The teams

Paul Gerrard, Michael Ball [Gary Naysmith], David Weir, Steve Watson, Alex Nyarko, Mark Pembridge*, Abel Xavier, Thomas Gravesen**, Idan Tal [Joe Max Moore], Paul Gascoigne, Kevin Campbell.

Sander Westerveld, Steven Gerrard, [Jamie Carragher], Christian Ziege, Sami Hyypia, Markus Babbel, Patrik Berger, Dietmar Hamann, Gary McAllister, Nick Barmby, Robbie Fowler [Vladimir Smicer], Emile Heskey.

*booked **sent off

● Campbell scores at Anfield to become the first Everton player since Andy King in 1978-79 and 1979-80, to score in this fixture in consecutive seasons.

● Thomas Gravesen's sending off is the first Everton dismissal of the season.

FA Premier League

Sunday 5 November 2000 • Goodison Park • Attendance 27,670
Kick-off 4pm • Referee SJ Lodge [Barnsley]

Everton 0	Aston Villa 1
	Merson 90

The teams

Paul Gerrard, Steve Watson [Scot Gemmill], David Weir, Abel Xavier*, David Unsworth* [Idan Tal], Thomas Gravesen, Paul Gascoigne [Danny Cadamarteri], Stephen Hughes, Mark Pembridge, Gary Naysmith*, Kevin Campbell.

David James, Alpay Oxzalan, Gareth Southgate, Gareth Barry, Steve Stone [Mark Delaney], George Boateng*, Ian Taylor, Alan Wright, Paul Merson, Gilles De Bilde [Darius Vassell*], Julian Joachim.

*booked **sent off

● Merson's goal, in the final minute, secures an undeserved win for the Midlands club, as it is their only shot on target.

FA Premier League

Saturday 11 November 2000 • Valley Park • Attendance 17,276
Kick-off 3pm • Referee RJ Harris [Oxford]

Bradford City 0

Everton 1
Naysmith 87

The teams

Paul Gerrard, David Weir, David Unsworth, Alex Nyarko, Kevin Campbell, Stephen Hughes* [Danny Cadamarteri], Mark Pembridge* [Scot Gemmill], Gary Naysmith, Thomas Gravesen, Abel Xavier, Idal Tal [Joe Max Moore].

Matt Clarke, Ian Nolan, Stuart McCall, David Wetherall, Gareth Whalley, Jamie Lawrence, Ashley Ward [Dean Saunders], Benito Carbone [Peter Beagrie], Peter Atherton, Dan Petrescu [Dean Windass], Stan Collymore.

*booked **sent off

● A late goal, by the former Hearts defender, Gary Naysmith, is his first for the club.

159

FA Premier League

Saturday 18 November 2000 • Goodison Park • Attendance 33,106
Kick-off 3pm • Referee MA Riley [Leeds]

Everton 2   Arsenal 0

Cadamarteri 54
Campbell 73

The teams

Paul Gerrard, Alec Cleland, Gary Naysmith, David Weir, Michael Ball, Mark Pembridge, Stephen Hughes, Scot Gemmill, Idan Tal [Kevin McLeod], Danny Cadamarteri, Kevin Campbell.

Alex Manninger, Lee Dixon* [Matthew Upson], Martin Keown, Oleg Luzhny, Ashley Cole, Freddie Ljungberg, Dennis Bergkamp, Ray Parlour, Robert Pires, Nwankwo Kanu, Sylvain Wiltord.

*booked **sent off

- Cadamarteri's first goal at Goodison since 18 October 1997, when he scored against Liverpool.

- Everton score from their only 2 shots at goal.

- Everton's first win against Arsenal since January 1996 and their first at Goodison in the Premiership.

FA Premier League

Saturday 25 November 2000 • Goodison Park • Attendance 33,515
Kick-off 3pm • Referee R Styles [Waterlooville]

Everton 2
Cadamarteri 47
Campbell 74

Chelsea 1
Dalla Bona 45

The teams

Paul Gerrard, Steve Watson, David Weir, Michael Ball, Gary Naysmith, Scot Gemmill, Mark Pembridge, Stephen Hughes, Idan Tal [David Unsworth], Kevin Campbell, Danny Cadamarteri [Kevin McLeod].

Ed de Goey, Frank Leboeuf, Marcel Desailly, Winston Bogarde [Gustavo Poyet], Mario Melchiot, Slavisa Jokanovic [Jody Morris], Dennis Wise, Samuele Dalla Bona, Eidur Gudjohnsen, Jimmy Floyd Hasselbaink**, Gianfranco Zola [Jon Harley].
*booked **sent off

- Cadamarteri continues his sequence of scoring against London clubs: his last 7 League goals have been against clubs from the capital.

FA Premier League

Monday 4 December 2000 • Stadium of Light • Attendance 46,372
Kick-off 8pm • Referee P Jones [Loughborough]

Sunderland 2
Rae 45
Phillips 65

Everton 0

The teams

Paul Gerrard, Steve Watson, David Weir, Kevin Campbell*, Stephen Hughes*, Mark Pembridge, Michael Ball, Gary Naysmith, Scot Gemmill [Alex Nyarko*], Danny Cadamarteri [Joe Max Moore], Idan Tal [Thomas Gravesen].

Thomas Sorensen, Darren Williams, Michael Gray, Gavin McCann, Emerson Thome, Jody Craddock, Kevin Kilbane, Kevin Phillips [John Oster], Niall Quinn [Stanislav Varga], Alex Rae [Stefan Schwarz], Julio Arca.
*booked **sent off

- A win would have given away victories in the same season against the North East 'big three' for the first time ever.

FA Premier League

Saturday 9 December 2000 • Maine Road • Attendance 34,516
Kick-off 3pm • Referee PR Richards [Preston]

Manchester City 5   Everton 0

Wanchope 14
Howey 23
Goater 42
Dickov 54
Naysmith [og] 67

The teams

Paul Gerrard, Steve Watson, David Weir, David Unsworth [Danny Cadamarteri], Gary Naysmith, Alex Nyarko*, Mark Pembridge, Scot Gemmill, Thomas Gravesen, Kevin Campbell, Michael Ball.

Nicky Weaver, Laurent Charvet, Danny Tiatto, Steve Howey, Richard Dunne, Alfie Haaland [Gerard Wiekens], Jeff Whitley, Kevin Horlock, Shaun Wright-Phillips [Mark Kennedy], Paolo Wanchope, Shaun Goater [Paul Dickov].

*booked **sent off

- Everton's heaviest ever Premiership loss and their biggest margin of defeat since the 5-0 derby defeat in November 1982.

- Joe Royle wins his first game as manager against the Blues since leaving in 1997.

- The previous visit to Manchester had seen a 5-1 loss at United in December 1999.

5 goals conceded in a Premiership match

0-5	Manchester City [a]	9 December 2000
1-5	Norwich City [h]	25 September 1993
1-5	Sheffield Wednesday [a]	2 April 1994
1-5	Manchester United [a]	4 December 1999
3-5	Queens Park Rangers [h]	12 April 1993

FA Premier League

Saturday 16 December 2000 • Goodison Park • Attendance 31,260
Kick-off 3pm • Referee CR Wilkes [Gloucester]

Everton 1
Cadamarteri 75

West Ham United 1
Kanoute 83

The teams

Paul Gerrard [Steve Simonsen], Steve Watson, David Weir, Stephen Hughes, Mark Pembridge, Michael Ball, Gary Naysmith, Thomas Gravesen [Niclas Alexandersson], Scot Gemmill, Danny Cadamarteri*, Kevin Campbell.

Shaka Hislop, Stuart Pearce, Rigobert Song, Ian Pearce, Trevor Sinclair, Steve Lomas*, Nigel Winterburn, Frank Lampard, Michael Carrick, Paolo Di Canio, Frederic Kanoute*.

*booked **sent off

- Memorable final minute sees Di Canio stop play in front of the Blue's goal, by catching the ball as it is crossed in, when keeper, Gerrard, is injured.

- Cadamarteri's 8th consecutive goal against London clubs.

FA Premier League

Saturday 23 December 2000 • The Valley • Attendance 20,043
Kick-off 3pm • Referee GP Barber [Tring]

Charlton Athletic 1
Svensson 9

Everton 0

The teams

Thomas Myhre, Steve Watson*, David Weir*, Michael Ball, Gary Naysmith, Niclas Alexandersson, Thomas Gravesen*, Scot Gemmill, Stephen Hughes [David Unsworth], Joe Max Moore [Idan Tal], Danny Cadamarteri [Duncan Ferguson].

Dean Kiely, Raddstin Kishishev [Paul Konchesky], Richard Rufus, Mark Fish [Steve Brown], Chris Powell, Graham Stuart*, Mark Kinsella, Claus Jensen, John Robinson, Jonatan Johansson [Martin Pringle], Mathias Svensson.

*booked **sent off

FA Premier League
Tuesday 26 December 2000 • Goodison Park • Attendance 35,704
Kick-off 3pm • Referee NS Barry [Scunthorpe]

Everton 1
Gemmill 85

Coventry 2
Hadji 69
Breen 87

The teams
Thomas Myhre, David Weir, Michael Ball, Gary Naysmith, Thomas Gravesen, Scot Gemmill, Mark Pembridge [Alex Nyarko], Idan Tal [David Unsworth], Duncan Ferguson*, Danny Cadamarteri* [Joe Max Moore].

Chris Kirkland, Gary Breen*, Paul Williams, Mo Konjic [Mark Edworthy], Barry Quinn, David Thompson, Paul Telfer, Lee Carsley, Craig Bellamy [Youssef Chippo], Mustapha Hadji, Ysrael Zuniga [John Alosi].

*booked **sent off

● This home defeat completes the worst December in the history of the club.

Worst League playing record in a calendar month

	P	L	D
March 1981	5	5	
November 1997	5	5	
September 1950	7	6	1
March 1930	5	4	1
November 1952	5	4	1
October 1994	5	4	1
December 2000	5	4	1

● The match against Leeds United, on 30 December, at home, was postponed due to bad weather, the first home postponement due to bad weather since the match against Southampton in January 1982.

FA Premier League
Monday 1 January 2001 • Pride Park • Attendance 27,358
Kick-off 3pm • Referee AG Wiley [Burntwood]

Derby County 1   Everton 0
Burton 20

The teams
Thomas Myhre, Steve Watson, David Weir*, Michael Ball, Scot Gemmill, Alex Nyarko* [Joe Max Moore], Thomas Gravesen* [David Unsworth], Mark Pembridge, Gary Naysmith, Duncan Ferguson, Niclas Alexandersson [Idan Tal].

Mart Poom, Rory Delap, Chris Riggott, Taribo West*, Horacio Carbonari*, Danny Higginbottam, Craig Burley [Adam Murray], Stefano Eranio [Georgi Kinkladze], Seth Johnson, Malcolm Christie, Deon Burton.

*booked **sent off

● 5 defeats in 6 games is the worst Premiership run since 1997-98.

FA Cup 3rd Round
Saturday 6 January 2001 • Vicarage Road • Attendance 15,635
Kick-off 3pm • Referee R Styles [Waterlooville]

Watford 1   Everton 2
Mooney 21   Hughes 82
                                 Watson 90

The teams
Thomas Myhre, Steve Watson*, Michael Ball, Mark Pembridge* [Idan Tal], David Weir, Gary Naysmith, Niclas Alexandersson, Stephen Hughes*, Thomas Gravesen [Scot Gemill], Danny Cadamarteri [Joe Max Moore**], Duncan Ferguson.

Alec Chamberlain, Neil Cox, Peter Kennedy [Steve Palmer], Paul Robinson, Darren Ward, Robert Page**, Paulo Vernazza, Allan Nielsen, Tommy Mooney, Tommy Smith, Clifton Noel-Williams [Heidar Helguson].

*booked **sent off

● Everton are now unbeaten in 12 away games at the 3rd Round stage since 1982, when the Blues lost 2-1 at West Ham.

FA Premier League
Saturday 13 January 2001 • Goodison Park • Attendance 32,290
Kick-off 3pm • Referee AP D'Urso [Billericay]

Everton 0   Tottenham Hotspur 0

The teams
Thomas Myhre, Steve Watson, David Weir [Alec Cleland], Michael Ball, David Unsworth, Niclas Alexandersson [Idan Tal], Thomas Gravesen, Mark Pembridge, Stephen Hughes*, Kevin Campbell, Joe Max Moore [Danny Cadamarteri].

Neil Sullivan, Chris Perry, Luke Young, Ledley King, Stephen Clemence, Gary Doherty, Tim Sherwood, Darren Anderton, Oyvind Leonhardsen [Simon Davies], Sergei Rebrov, Willem Korsten [David McEwen].

*booked **sent off

- First goalless draw of the season and the first in 25 League games since the derby in April 2000.

FA Premier League
Saturday 20 January 2001 • Highfield Road • Attendance 19,174
Kick-off • Referee • PA Durkin [Portland]

Coventry City 1   Everton 3
Carsley [pen] 86   Gemmill 8
                                            Cadamarteri 15
                                            Campbell 31

The teams
Thomas Myhre, Steve Watson, Michael Ball, David Unsworth, Alec Cleland, [Peter Clarke], Idan Tal, Scot Gemmill*, Niclas Alexandersson [Phil Jevoni], Mark Pembridge, Kevin Campbell, Danny Cadamarteri.

Chris Kirkland, Mark Edworthy, Barry Quinn, Gary Breen, Mo Konjic [Carlton Palmer], David Thompson, John Eustace, Lee Carsley, Paul Telfer [Youssef Chippo], Ysrael Zuniga [John Aloisi], Mustapha Hadji.

*booked **sent off

- The Blues' tally of 3 goals in the opening half hour, is more than they had managed in the previous 10 hours of Premiership football.
- Cadamarteri's first League goal against a team outside of London since October 1997.

FA Cup 4th Round
Saturday 27 January 2001 • Goodison Park • Attendance 39,207
Kick-off • Referee • JT Winter [Stockton-on-Tees]

Everton 0

Tranmere Rovers 3
Yates 32, 63
Koumas 35

The teams

Thomas Myhre, Steve Watson, Abel Xavier, Michael Ball, David Unsworth [Richard Gough], Thomas Gravesen*, Mark Pembridge*, Scot Gemmill*, Stephen Hughes [Joe Max Moore], Danny Cadamarteri [Idan Tal], Kevin Campbell.

John Achterberg, Richard Jobson, Graham Allen*, Clint Hill, Steve Yates, Sean Flynn [Nick Henry], Jason Koumas, Des Hamilton, Richard Hinds, Paul Rideout [Ian Hume], Andy Parkinson [Scott Taylor].

*booked **sent off

● Three of the 4 worst home defeats in the FA Cup have come against clubs from lower divisions.

● The previous player to score twice against Everton in the FA Cup at Goodison was Peter Beardsley for Liverpool in 1991.

Heaviest defeats at home in the FA Cup

v	Crystal Palace*	0-6	7 January 1922	1st Round
v	Liverpool*	0-4	29 January 1955	4th Round
v	Aston Villa	1-4	14 February 1959	5th Round
v	Tranmere Rovers*	0-3	27 January 2001	4th Round

*side from a lower division

FA Premier League

Wednesday 31 January 2001 • Goodison Park • Attendance 34,244
Kick-off 7.45pm • Referee GP Barber [Tring]

Everton 2
Naysmith 49
Tal 79

Middlesbrough 2
Ricard 11
Cooper 63

The teams

Thomas Myhre, Steve Watson*, Richard Gough, David Weir, Michael Ball, Gary
Naysmith, Scot Gemmill, Thomas Gravesen [Idan Tal], Duncan Ferguson, Joe Max Moore
[Abel Xavier], Kevin Campbell.

Mark Schwarzer*, Curtis Fleming, Steve Vickers*, Colin Cooper*, Ugo Ehiogu*, Dean
Gordon* [Gianluco Festa], Paul Ince*, Paul Okon, Christian Karembeu [Robbie Mustoe],
Alen Boksic, Hamilton Ricard [Phil Whelan].
*booked **sent off

● Idan Tal scores his first goal for the club.

FA Premier League

Saturday 3 February 2001 • Old Trafford • Attendance 67,528
Kick-off 3pm • Referee JT Winter [Stockton-on-Tees]

Manchester United 1
Cole 52

Everton 0

The teams

Paul Gerrard, David Weir, Richard Gough, Michael Ball, Steve Watson, Thomas
Gravesen*, Scot Gemmill*, Gary Naysmith [David Unsworth], Joe Max Moore [Danny
Cadamarteri], Kevin Campbell, Idan Tal [Phil Jevons].

Fabien Barthez, Dennis Irwin, Wes Brown, Jaap Stam, Mikael Silvestre, Luke Chadwick
[Teddy Sheringham], David Beckham [Ron Wallwork], Paul Scholes [Ryan Giggs], Phil
Neville, Andy Cole, Dwight Yorke.
*booked **sent off

● United score with their only shot on target in the entire game.

● Everton have now lost 10 and drawn 2 of the last 12 Premiership meetings with
Ferguson's men.

● Highest ever attendance at an Everton away game in the League.

FA Premier League

Wednesday 7 February 2001 • Goodison Park • Attendance 34,224
Kick-off 8pm • Referee NS Barry [Scunthorpe]

Everton 2

Ferguson 23
Campbell 73

Leeds United 2

Harte 66
Dacourt 76

The teams

Paul Gerrard, Michael Ball, Richard Gough, David Weir, Gary Naysmith*, Scot Gemmill*, Thomas Gravesen*, Steve Watson, Joe Max Moore [David Unsworth], Kevin Campbell, Duncan Ferguson [Idan Tal].

Nigel Martyn, Ian Harte, Lucas Radebe*, Rio Ferdinand, Danny Mills, Dominic Matteo [Jason Wilcox], David Batty, Olivier Dacourt, Lee Bowyer [Eirik Bakke], Mark Viduka, Robbie Keane [Alan Smith].

*booked **sent off

● Former player, Olivier Dacourt, hits equaliser.

FA Premier League

Saturday 10 February 2001 • Goodison Park • Attendance 30,409
Kick-off 3pm • Referee R Styles [Waterlooville]

Everton 2
Jeffers 8
Campbell 43

Leicester City 1
Sturridge 79

The teams

Paul Gerrard, Steve Watson, Gary Naysmith, Michael Ball, Richard Gough [David Unsworth*], David Weir, Stephen Hughes [Joe Max Moore*], Scot Gemmill, Thomas Gravesen, Francis Jeffers [Danny Cadamarteri], Kevin Campbell.

Simon Royce, Gary Rowett*, Matt Elliott, Gerry Taggart [Frank Sinclair], Andy Impey*, Matthew Jones [Roberto Mancini], Robbie Savage, Muzzy Izzet, Junior Lewis, Steve Guppy [Darren Eadie], Dean Sturridge.

*booked **sent off

- First home win for 6 League games.

- Cadamarteri's 58th appearance, as a substitute for the club, is a new Everton record [see Everton appearances for list].

- Dean Sturridge scores at Goodison for the 2nd time in the season, he had scored against the Blues for the derby in August 2000.

FA Premier League
Saturday 24 February 2001 • Portman Road • Attendance 22,220
Kick-off 3pm • Referee G Poll [Tring]

Ipswich Town 2
Holland 82
Armstrong 84

Everton 0

The teams
Paul Gerrard, David Weir, Alex Nyarko**, Stephen Hughes, Michael Ball, Francis Jeffers [Kevin McLeod], Gary Naysmith, Thomas Gravesen, Abel Xavier*, Idan Tal [Phil Jevons], Kevin Campbell.

Richard Wright, Fabian Wilnis [Alun Armstrong], Jamie Clapham, John McGreal, Mark Venus [Martyn Reuser], Titus Bramble, Jim Magilton [Nabil Abdallah], Matt Holland, James Scowcroft, Mark Burchill, Jermaine Wright.
*booked **sent off

● Nyarko sent off for the first time in his Everton career.

FA Premier League
Saturday 3 March 2001 • Goodison Park • Attendance 35,779
Kick-off 3pm • Referee D Elleray [Harrow-on-the-Hill]

Everton 1
Unsworth [pen] 82

Newcastle United 1
Unsworth [og] 47

The teams
Paul Gerrard, Abel Xavier [Paul Gascoigne], David Weir, Michael Ball, Steve Watson, Gary Naysmith* [David Unsworth], Scot Gemmill, Alex Nyarko [Idan Tal], Thomas Gravesen, Kevin Campbell, Francis Jeffers.

Shay Given, Andrew Griffin, Stephen Caldwell, Aaron Hughes, Wayne Quinn, Christian Bassedas [Stephen Glass], Robert Lee*, Clarence Acuna, Nolberto Solano [Daniel Cordone], Alan Shearer*, Foluwashola Ameobi [Kevin Gallagher].
*booked **sent off

● David Unsworth is the first Everton player since Mike Newell, at Southampton in 1991, to score at both ends, one of the few instances in the history of the game when a substitute has achieved this feat.

FA Premier League
Saturday 17 March 2001 • The Dell • Attendance 15,251
Kick-off 3pm • Referee M Halsey [Welwyn Garden City]

Southampton 1   Everton 0
Tessem 58

The teams
Paul Gerrard, Steve Watson, David Weir, Michael Ball, Abel Xavier, Thomas Gravesen, Scot Gemmill [David Unsworth], Mark Pembridge [Alessandro Pistone*], Duncan Ferguson, Niclas Alexandersson [Paul Gascoigne].

Paul Jones, Claus Lundekvam, Dean Richards, Tahar El Khalej [Jason Dodd], Dan Petrescu, Wayne Bridge*, Matthew Oakley, Mark Draper, Jo Tessem, Marian Pahars, James Beattie*.

*booked **sent off

FA Premier League
Saturday 31 March 2001 • Upton Park • Attendance 26, 044
Kick-off 3pm • Referee AP D'Urso [Billericay]

West Ham United 0   Everton 2
                                        Unsworth [pen] 45
                                        Alexandersson 71

The teams
Paul Gerrard, Steve Watson, David Weir, David Unsworth*, Niclas Alexandersson, Alex Nyarko, Michael Ball*, Thomas Gravesen [Francis Jeffers], Scot Gemmill, Duncan Ferguson, Anthony Hibbert.

Shaka Hislop, Stuart Pearce**, Rigobert Song, Igor Stimac, Hayden Foxe, Nigel Winterburn, Michael Carrick, Joe Cole, Frank Lampard, Paolo Di Canio, Frederic Kanoute.

*booked **sent off

- Unsworth scores a penalty against his former club.
- Upton Park is one of the club's favourite grounds, with 3 wins and 3 draws in the last 8 visits.

FA Premier League

Sunday 8 April 2001 • Goodison Park • Attendance 36,561
Kick-off 3pm • Referee D Elleray [Harrow-on-the-Hill]

Everton 3

Ferguson 16
Ball 40
Weir 84

Manchester City 1

Whitley 9

The teams

Paul Gerrard, Steve Watson, David Weir, Michael Ball, Alessandro Pistone**, Niclas Alexandersson [Idan Tal], Scot Gemmill, Thomas Gravesen, David Unsworth, Kevin Campbell, Duncan Ferguson [Francis Jeffers] [Mark Pembridge].

Nicky Weaver*, Alfie Haaland, Steve Howey, Richard Dunne, Danny Granville [Mark Kennedy], Andrei Kanchelskis [Darren Huckerby] Gerard Wiekens, Jeff Whitley*, Danny Tiatto*, Paul Dickov**, Paolo Wanchope.

*booked **sent off

● Michael Ball missed Everton's 3rd penalty penalty awarded in 4 matches, but scored the rebound.

FA Premier League

Saturday 14 April 2001 • Villa Park • Attendance • 31,272
Kick-off 3pm • Referee P Taylor [Cheshunt]

Aston Villa 2
Dublin 2
Taylor 81

Everton 1
Unsworth 21

The teams

Paul Gerrard, Steve Watson, David Weir, David Unsworth [Joe Max Moore], Michael Ball*, Niclas Alexandersson [Idan Tal], Scot Gemmill, Thomas Gravesen* [Alex Nyarko], Mark Pembridge, Alessandro Pistone*, Kevin Campbell.

David James, Mark Delaney, Gareth Southgate, Alpay Ozalan, Alan Wright, Steve Stone [Darius Vassell], Ian Taylor, George Boateng, Paul Merson, Lee Hendrie [David Ginola], Dion Dublin [Juan Pablo Angel].

*booked **sent off

- For the 2nd time in a fortnight, Unsworth scores against a former club.
- 9 goals, in 18 Premiership games against Villa, is the worst ratio against any club.
- No win at Villa Park in the League since Easter Saturday 1987.

Goal ratio

Ratio of goals scored per game by Everton in the Premiership [minimum 14 games].

Highest

West Ham United	31 goals	16 games	1.93 ratio of goals per game
Wimbledon	28 goals	16 games	1.75 ratio of goals per game
Chelsea	24 goals	18 games	1.33 ratio of goals per game

Lowest

Aston Villa	9 goals	18 games	0.50 ratio of goals per game
Arsenal	11 goals	18 games	0.61 ratio of goals per game
Manchester United	13 goals	18 games	0.72 ratio of goals per game

FA Premier League
Monday 16 April 2001 • Goodison Park • Attendance 40,260
Kick-off 6pm • Referee JT Winter [Stockton-on-Tees]

Everton 2
Ferguson 42
Unsworth [pen] 84

Liverpool 3
Heskey 5
Babbel 57
McAllister 90

The teams
Paul Gerrard*, David Weir, Richard Gough* [Niclas Alexandersson*], Michael Ball*, Steve Watson [Alessandro Pistone], David Unsworth*, Abel Xavier, Alex Nyarko, Scot Gemmill, Kevin Campbell, Duncan Ferguson*.

Sander Westerveld, Markus Babbel, Stepahne Henchoz*, Sami Hyypia, Jamie Carragher*, Vladimir Smicer, Dietmar Hamann*, Gary McAllister*, Igor Biscan**, Emile Heskey, Robbie Fowler [Gregory Vignal].

*booked **sent off

- 11 players booked and Igor Biscan sent off for Liverpool.
- For the first time both sides are awarded a penalty in a derby.
- Unsworth's spot kick is the first Everton penalty success in a home derby since Roy Vernon in 1962.
- Robbie Fowler's missed penalty is the first for Liverpool since 1985.
- Biggest Premiership crowd at Goodison.
- First Everton defeat in a weekday League derby game for 13 matches in 23 years.

FA Premier League
Saturday 21 April 2001 • Highbury • Attendance 38,029
Kick-off 3pm • Referee DJ Gallagher [Banbury]

Arsenal 4
Ljungberg 21
Grimaldi 55
Wiltord 67
Henry 87

Everton 1
Campbell 24

The teams
Paul Gerrard, Michael Ball, David Weir, Alessandro Pistone, Abel Xavier**, Scot Gemmill, Thomas Gravesen, Alex Nyarko [Idan Tal], Mark Pembridge [Anthony Hibbert], Niclas Alexandersson [Joe Max Moore], Kevin Campbell.

David Seaman, Lee Dixon, Martin Keown, Tony Adams, Ashley Cole, Robert Pires [Silvinho], Gilles Grimandi [Nelson Vivas], Patrick Vieira, Freddie Ljungberg, Sylvain Wiltord, Thierry Henry.

*booked **sent off

- Campbell's goal means he has scored against his former club in both League matches in 2000-01.

FA Premier League
Saturday 28 April 2001 • Goodison Park • Attendance 34,256
Kick-off 3pm • Referee PA Durkin [Portland]

Everton 2
Ferguson 47
Alexandersson 64

Bradford City 1
Myers 2

The teams
Paul Gerrard, David Unsworth* [Thomas Gravesen], Michael Ball, Richard Gough [Anthony Hibbert], David Weir, Steve Watson, Mark Pembridge, Scot Gemmill, Niclas Alexandersson, Duncan Ferguson, Kevin Campbell.

Gary Walsh, Wayne Jacobs, Andy Myers, Robert Molenaar, Gunnar Halle, Eion Jess, Robbie Blake, Stuart McCall, Jamie Lawrence, Ashley Ward*, Benito Carbone.

*booked **sent off

- For the only time in the season, Everton win after going a goal down at home.
- Bradford miss 2 penalties, through Blake and Carbone, the first instance against Everton in the Premiership.

FA Premier League
Saturday 5 May 2001 • Stamford Bridge • Attendance 35,196
Kick-off 3pm • Referee R Styles [Waterlooville]

Chelsea 2	Everton 1
Hasselbaink 31, 33	Campbell 1

The teams
Paul Gerrard, Steve Watson, David Weir, Michael Ball, David Unsworth, Niclas Alexandersson [Gary Naysmith], Scot Gemmill*, Mark Pembidge [Kevin McLeod], Idan Tal, Kevin Campbell, Joe Max Moore [Phil Jevons].

Carlo Cudicini, Mario Melchiot, John Terry*, Marcel Desailly, Graeme Le Saux, Gianfrance Zola [Slavisa Jokanovic], Jody Morris, Dennis Wise, Gustavo Poyet [Celestine Babayaro], Eidur Gudjohnsen [Jesper Gronkjaer], Jimmy Floyd Hasselbaink.
*booked **sent off

● Campbell's first minute goal is the quickest of the season and his 30th goal in his 62nd League appearance.

● Kevin McLeod makes his 5th and final substitute appearance of the season without making a start for the first team.

Fewest games to reach 30 League goals in the top-flight from 1954

Fred Pickering	37
Gary Lineker	41
Roy Vernon	51
Joe Royle	61
Kevin Campbell	62

Most substitute appearances in Everton career without starting a game

Warren Aspinall	8	1986 – 1987
Kevin McLeod	5	2000 – 2001
Jamie Milligan	4	1998 – 2000
Tommy Johnson	2	1998 – 1999

FA Premier League

Saturday 19 May 2001 • Goodison Park • Attendance 37,444
Kick-off 3pm • Referee SG Bennett [Orpington]

Everton 2

Tal 9
Ball 75 [pen]

Sunderland 2

Phillips 20, 83

The teams

Paul Gerrard*, Gary Naysmith, David Unsworth, Michael Ball*, David Weir*, Steve Watson, Idan Tal* [Danny Cadamarteri], Scot Gemmill, Mark Pembridge, Thomas Gravesen* [Niclas Alexandersson], Kevin Campbell.

Thomas Sorensen, Michael Gray [Darren Williams], Emerson Thome, Jody Craddock*, Patrice Cateron, Kevin Kilbane*, Stefan Schwarz*, Gavin McCann, Julio Arca [Don Hutchison**], Kevin Phillips, Niall Quinn [Kevin Kyle].

*booked **sent off

- Don Hutchison sent off, making him the first player to be sent off both playing for and against Everton in the Premiership.

- Unsworth misses a penalty and Ball scores a second kick – 8 penalties awarded in the last 5 home games of the season.

Penalties in Everton Premiership matches in 2000-01 season

Sergi Rebrov	for Tottenham Hotspur [a]	5 September 2000
Michael Ball	v Southampton [h]	14 October 2000
Patrik Berger	for Liverpool [a]	29 October 2000
Lee Carsley	for Coventry City [a]	20 January 2001
David Unsworth	v Newcastle United [h]	3 March 2001
David Unsworth	v West Ham United [a]	31 March 2001
Michael Ball*	v Manchester City [h]	8 April 2001
Robbie Fowler*	for Liverpool [h]	16 April 2001
David Unsworth	v Liverpool [h]	16 April 2001
Robbie Blake*	for Bradford City [h]	28 April 2001
Benito Carbone*	for Bradford City [h]	28 April 2001
David Unsworth*	v Sunderland [h]	19 May 2001
Michael Ball	v Sunderland [h]	19 May 2001

*missed

2000-01 season – Premiership facts and figures

- Everton finished 16th in the Premiership.
- Kevin Campbell, leading Premiership scorer for the 3rd consecutive season, [9 goals].
- The only side which Everton beat home and away was Bradford City.
- The following sides defeated Everton both home and away: Manchester United, Ipswich Town, Liverpool and Aston Villa.
- The biggest win was the 3-0 win over Charlton in August.
- The most consecutive wins were the 3 achieved in November against Bradford, Arsenal and Chelsea.
- The average home League attendance was 34,111, and the average for all Premiership matches involving the Blues was 33,142 per game, the highest average for Everton games in the top-flight since 1977-78.
- More penalties were awarded at Goodison, 9 in total, than at any other Premiership ground.

EVERTON IN THE PREMIERSHIP

The Premier League

Since the introduction of the Premiership, in 1992-93, there has been a plethora of statistics solely devoted to the new top-flight. Sadly, in times to come, it will be inevitable that there will be a distinction between the old 1st Division and the new Premier League in collating the statistics of players and clubs.

However, it would be slightly remiss to ignore the new format – especially for younger fans – and what follows are key facts and feats relating to Everton's tenure in what has become the most popular league on the planet.

Premiership record

Everton was one of the 3 founder members of the Football League [with Aston Villa and Blackburn Rovers] who were also founder members of the Premier League in 1992-93.

Everton's consolidated Premiership record to the end of 2000-01

	P	W	D	L	For	Against	Points
Home	177	66	58	53	254	208	256
Away	177	42	43	92	180	273	169
Total	354	108	101	145	434	481	425

- Everton's best season was in 1995-96, when they finished 6th. In 1993-94 and 1997-98, the club finished in 17th position, on both occasions famously surviving at Goodison on the final day of the season.

- In that time, Howard Kendall, Mike Walker, Joe Royle, Howard Kendall [again] and Walter Smith, have managed the club on a permanent basis.

Most appearances

Dave Watson	223
David Unsworth	210
Neville Southall	207
Andy Hinchcliffe	143
Graham Stuart	136
Duncan Ferguson	128
Barry Horne	123
John Ebbrell	121
Michael Ball	121
Nicky Barmby	116
Paul Rideout	112
Gary Ablett	111
Matt Jackson	108

- At the beginning of the 2001-02 season the only current Everton player to have appeared for the Blues in the old First Division and the Premiership is David Unsworth.

Most goals in the Premiership

Duncan Ferguson	43
Kevin Campbell	30
Paul Rideout	29
Tony Cottee	28
David Unsworth	23
Graham Stuart	22
Andrei Kanchelskis	20
Nick Barmby	18
Francis Jeffers	18
Gary Speed	17
Danny Cadamarteri	13

- Two players have scored 16 Premiership goals in a season: Tony Cottee in 1993-94 and Andrei Kanchelskis in 1995-96.

- Everton's first Premiership goal was scored by Barry Horne against Sheffield Wednesday at Goodison on the opening day of the 1992-93 season.

- The following players have each scored in a record 4 consecutive Premiership games for the Blues: Andrei Kanchelskis 17 March – 6 April 1996, Kevin Campbell 23 October – 20 November 1999 and Francis Jeffers 23 August – 9 September 2000.

Premiership opponents

- In the 18 games against Arsenal, the Blues' only victories came on 20 January 1996, when they won 2-1 at Highbury, and on 18 November 2000 at Goodison in a 2-0 win.

- In the 18 games against Aston Villa, the club's only 2 wins came in the very first Premier League game staged at Goodison in 1992, by 1-0, and also by 1-0 at Goodison, in May 1996.

- In the 18 Premiership matches against Leeds, the away side has yet to record a victory. Leeds have drawn 5 and lost 4 at Goodison and the Blues have drawn 3 and lost 6 at Elland Road.

- Leicester's only victory in the Premiership came at Filbert Street, in August 1998.

- Everton won the first meeting with Manchester United, 3-0, on 19 August 1992. The only win in the 17 games since, came on 25 February 1995, at Goodison, with Duncan Ferguson heading the only goal of the game.

- The Blues failed to win one of the first 7 meetings with Sheffield Wednesday, before winning 5-2 at Hillsborough, on 27 April 1996, when Andrei Kanchelskis scored a hat trick. Wednesday have lost only one of their 8 visits to Goodison.

- One of the club's bogey sides continues to be Tottenham, as the Blues have only beaten the Londoners once in 18 fixtures, on 12 April 1997, with Gary Speed scoring the only goal.

Premiership results
Everton's biggest wins in the Premiership.

7-1	v Southampton (h)	16 November 1996
6-0	v West Ham United (h)	8 May 1999
6-2	v Swindon Town (h)	15 January 1994

- The best away wins are 5-2 at Manchester City on 8 May 1993 and at Sheffield Wednesday on 27 April 1996.

- The biggest margin of victory, away from home, is the 4-0 win at West Ham United on 26 February 2000.

First Premiership win
- The Blues first win was at Old Trafford in a 3-0 victory on 19 August 1992. This remains United's worst home defeat in the Premiership.

Consecutive wins
- The record for most consecutive Everton wins for in the Premiership is 4, achieved in the final game of the 1992-93 season and the first three matches of the 1993-94 campaign.

Unbeaten sequence
- Everton set a Premiership record, for the club, of 8 games unbeaten from 14 April 1995 to 19 August 1995.

Biggest defeats
- The biggest defeat in the Premiership is the 5-0 loss at Maine Road, against Manchester City, on 9 December 2000

Most consecutive defeats
- Six consecutive defeats were suffered from 26 December 1996 to 29 January 1997.

Sequence of games without a win
- The Blues went a record 12 consecutive games (4 draws and 8 defeats) without a Premiership win from the start of the 1994-95 season.

Sent off

All these players have been dismissed in Premier League games involving Everton. The names of the Everton players are in *italics*.

1992-93	*Neville Southall*	v	Queens Park Rangers	28 December 1992
	Paul Rideout	v	Queens Park Rangers	28 December 1992
	Neville Southall	v	Sheffield Wednesday	6 February 1993
	Tim Sherwood	for	Blackburn	3 March 1993
	Andy Kernaghan	for	Middlesbrough	10 April 1993
1993-94	Andy Mutch	for	Swindon	15 January 1994
	Graeme Sharp	for	Oldham	5 March 1994
1994-95	Steve Chettle	for	Nottingham Forest	30 August 1994
	Duncan Ferguson	v	Arsenal	14 January 1995
	Earl Barrett	v	Newcastle United	1 February 1995
	Barry Horne	v	Newcastle United	1 February 1995
	Vinny Samways	v	Leicester City	4 March 1995 ⎱ same
	Duncan Ferguson	v	Leicester City	4 March 1995 ⎰ game
	Terry Phelan	v	Manchester City	15 March 1995
	Robert Lee	for	Newcastle United	14 April 1995
	Stuart Barlow	v	Ipswich Town	9 May 1995
1995-96	*David Unsworth*	v	Manchester United	9 September 1995
	Richard Sneekes	for	Bolton Wanderers	14 October 1995
	Barry Horne	v	Bolton Wanderers	14 October 1995
	Ludek Miklosko	for	West Ham United	11 December 1995
	John Beresford	for	Newcastle United	16 December 1995
	David Watson	v	Leeds United	30 December 1995
	Mark Hughes	for	Chelsea	13 January 1996
	Michael Frontzeck	for	Manchester City	10 February 1996
	Gary Flitcroft	for	Blackburn Rovers	30 March 1996
1996-97	*Duncan Ferguson*	v	Blackburn Rovers	21 September 1996
	David Unsworth	v	Liverpool	12 April 1997
	Robbie Fowler	for	Liverpool	12 April 1997
	Frode Grodas	for	Chelsea	11 May 1997
1997-98	*Andy Hinchcliffe*	v	Derby County	13 September 1997
	Slaven Bilic	v	Newcastle United	24 September 1997
	Slaven Bilic	v	Chelsea	26 November 1997
	Duncan Ferguson	v	Derby County	14 February 1998
	Slaven Bilic	v	Southampton	7 March 1998
	Ken Monkou	for	Southampton	7 March 1998
	Lucas Radebe	for	Leeds United	11 April 1998
	Andy Booth	for	Sheffield Wednesday	25 April 1998

1998-99	Olivier Dacourt	v	Leeds United	12 September 1998
	Martin Dahlin	for	Blackburn Rovers	26 September 1998
	Dennis Wise	for	Chelsea	5 December 1998
	Richard Dunne	v	Chelsea	5 December 1998
	Alec Cleland	v	Aston Villa	18 January 1999
	Emmanuel Petit	for	Arsenal	13 March 1999
	Don Hutchison	v	Arsenal	13 March 1999
	Marco Materazzi	v	Coventry City	11 April 1999
1999-00	John Collins	v	Aston Villa	11 August 1999
	Richard Dunne	v	Derby County	28 August 1999
	Sander Westerveld	for	Liverpool	22 September 1999
	Steven Gerrard	for	Liverpool	27 September 1999
	Francis Jeffers	v	Liverpool	27 September 1999
	David Weir	v	Middlesbrough	30 October 1999
	Frank Leboeuf	for	Chelsea	20 November 1999
	Neil Cox	for	Watford	18 December 1999
	Michael Duberry	for	Leeds United	8 March 2000
	Richard Dunne	v	Leeds United	8 May 2000
	Don Hutchison	v	Leeds United	8 May 2000
2000-01	Carl Tiler	for	Charlton	23 August 2000
	Thomas Gravesen	v	Liverpool	29 October 2000
	Jimmy Floyd Hasselbaink	for	Chelsea	25 November 2000
	Alex Nyarko	v	Ipswich Town	24 February 2001
	Stuart Pearce	for	West Ham	31 March 2001
	Paul Dickov	for	Manchester City*	8 April 2001
	Alessandro Pistone	v	Manchester City	8 April 2001
	Igor Biscan	for	Liverpool	16 April 2001
	Abel Xavier	v	Arsenal	21 April 2001
	Don Hutchison	for	Sunderland	19 May 2001

* later reduced to caution

Former Blues sent off in the Premiership against Everton

Graeme Sharp	Oldham [h]	5 March 1994
Carl Tiler	Charlton Athletic [h]	23 August 2000
Don Hutchison	Sunderland [h]	19 May 2001

Premiership own goals for Everton

Ian Brightwell	Manchester City [h]	31 October 1992
Colin Hendry	Blackburn Rovers [h]	3 March 1993
Phil Whelan	Ipswich Town [a]	30 October 1993
Alan McDonald	Queens Park Rangers [a]	18 March 1995
David Wetherall	Leeds United [h]	30 December 1995
Neil Ruddock	Liverpool [h]	18 October 1997
Michael Duberry	Chelsea [h]	18 January 1998
Jaap Stam	Manchester United [h]	8 August 1999
Claus Lundekvam	Southampton [h]	21 August 1999

Premiership own goals against Everton

Dave Watson	v Leeds United [a]	30 April 1994
Gary Ablett	v Wimbledon [h]	7 May 1994
Andy Hinchcliffe	v Nottingham Forest [h]	30 August 1994
Dave Watson	v Nottingham Forest [a]	17 September 1995
David Unsworth	v Manchester United [a]	21 August 1996
Craig Short	v Southampton [a]	5 March 1997
Claus Thomsen	v Liverpool [h]	16 April 1997
Dave Watson	v West Ham United [h]	23 August 1997
Slaven Bilic	v Arsenal [a]	3 May 1998
Craig Short	v Manchester United [h]	31 October 1998
Dave Watson	v Tottenham Hotspur [h]	15 January 2000
Steve Watson	v Middlesbrough [a]	9 September 2000
Gary Naysmith	v Manchester City [a]	9 December 2000
Steve Watson	v Manchester United [a]	3 February 2001
David Unsworth	v Newcastle United [h]	3 March 2001

Premiership hat tricks

Tony Cottee	v Sheffield United [h]	21 August 1993
Tony Cottee	v Swindon Town [h]	15 January 1994
Andrei Kanchelskis	v Sheffield Wednesday [a]	27 April 1996
Gary Speed	v Southampton [h]	16 November 1996
Duncan Ferguson	v Bolton Wanderers [h]	28 December 1997
Kevin Campbell	v West Ham United [h]	8 May 1999
Nick Barmby	v West Ham United [a]	26 February 2000

EVERTON IN THE LEAGUE

Everton in the League

Everton have played more League matches in the top-flight than any other side, confirming their status as, historically, one of the biggest clubs in English football.

In order to do justice to that fact, the following pages look at Everton's performance against all the other clubs which the Blues have faced in the League.

The analysis is in 3 sections:

● The first section looks at Everton's record against each of the sides who make up the Premiership in the 2001-02 season [as well as the 3 sides who were relegated in 2000-01]. The analysis covers the playing record, winning and losing streaks, individual scoring records, sendings-off and hat tricks. Much of the information, especially relating to the opposition, is produced for the first time in any book.

● The second section takes a look at the individual scoring records and hat tricks, both for and against the other clubs which Everton have faced in League matches.

● The 3rd section looks at the records of individuals who have – perhaps unfortunately – made a habit of scoring goals against the Blues over the years. Some clubs' scoring records against Everton are not available.

ARSENAL

Head to head

Home	Everton	Won 35	Drew 21	Lost 24
Away	Everton	Won 16	Drew 13	Lost 51

Home

The victory in November 2000 was the Blues' first in 9 years at Goodison, the previous being a 3-1 win in August 1991.

Away

Everton have won only one of the last 14 visits – winning 2-1 in 1995-96 – and only 3 of the last 26 games at Highbury.

Overall

Everton have won only 4 of the last 28 games home and away.

Sent off

On 13 March 1999, Emmanuel Petit and Don Hutchison were both sent off at Goodison, whilst Abel Xavier received his marching orders at Highbury in April 2001.

Most goals for Everton

Dixie Dean	11
Roy Vernon	9
Alex Young	5
Adrian Heath	5

Everton hat tricks

Dixie Dean	1927-28
Roy Vernon	1960-61

Most goals for Arsenal

Ian Wright	12
David Herd	9
James Brain	8
Reg Lewis	7
Vic Groves	6

Arsenal hat tricks

James Brain	1925-26
James Brain	1925-26
Jack Lambert	1929-30
Ted Drake	1937-38
David Herd [4]	1958-59
David Herd	1960-61
Ian Wright [4]	1991-92

ASTON VILLA

Head to head

Home	Everton	Won 41	Drew 22	Lost 23
Away	Everton	Won 24	Drew 19	Lost 43

Home

At Goodison, Everton have not won in the last 5 League games, with their last win coming on the final day of the season in May 1996, when Joe Parkinson scored the last of his 3 League goals for the Blues in a 1-0 victory.

Away

Everton have lost the last 6 visits to Villa Park and have not won in the last 13 meetings there, scoring only 8 goals. Everton's last win at Villa Park came on 18 April 1987, when Kevin Sheedy scored in a 1-0 win.

The last occasion Everton conceded 6 goals, in any League match, was a 6-2 defeat on the ground in November 1989.

Overall

The 172 League meetings are a record for English football.
Villa have lost only 2 of the last 21 meetings home and away.

Sent off

The last sending-off was John Collins, at Villa Park, in 1999-00, although Benito Carbone was sent off in the FA Cup, at Goodison, in March 2000. Collins has unhappy memories of meetings between the sides, for he missed from the spot against Villa on the opening day of the season in 1998, Walter Smith's first game in charge.

Most goals for Everton

Dixie Dean	19
Fred Geary	9
Graeme Sharp	8
Roy Vernon	6

Everton hat tricks

John Bell	1895-96
Bobby Parker	1914-15
Bobby Irvine	1921-22
Dixie Dean	1927-28

Most goals for Aston Villa

Harry Hampton	14
Billy Walker	11
Dai Astley	8
Johnny Dixon	8

Aston Villa hat tricks

Len Capewell	1926-27
George Brown	1929-30

BLACKBURN ROVERS

Head to head

Home	Everton	Won 35	Drew 14	Lost 14
Away	Everton	Won 15	Drew 13	Lost 35

Home

Everton have won only 3 of the last 11 encounters, with only 2 victories in the 7 Premiership matches.

Away

The Blues have won all 7 of the last 13 visits to Ewood Park.

Overall

Everton have won only one more game than Blackburn in the series – 50 against 49. In the Premiership, the series is tied, at 6 wins apiece.
Everton's last League game before the War was a 2-2 draw against Blackburn, on 2 September 1939.

Sent off

Martin Dahlin of Rovers was the last player sent off in the fixture, in September 1998.

Most goals for Everton

Dixie Dean	16

Everton hat tricks

Alex Young	1910-11
Dixie Dean	1931-32
Tom Johnson	1932-33
Tommy White	1933-34

Most goals for Blackburn

Alan Shearer	7

Blackburn hat tricks

W Davies [4]	1908-09
H Latheron	1913-14
John McIntyre [4]	1922-23
J Smith	1946-47
Fred Pickering	1963-64

- McIntyre's 4 goals came in a League record 5-minute spell.
- Pickering would later move to Everton in the same season and scored a hat trick on his Blues debut against Nottingham Forest.

BOLTON WANDERERS

Head to head

Home	Everton	Won	35	Drew	16	Lost	7
Away	Everton	Won	24	Drew	11	Lost	23

Home

The last meeting, on 27 December 1997, saw a Duncan Ferguson hat trick of headers in a 3-2 win. Bolton's last victory at Goodison was on 4 February 1961.

Away

One of the few grounds on which the Blues have a superior record to their opponents. However, the last win was a 3-1 victory, in September 1963. Bolton's last victory was also 3-1, on 3 April 1979.

Most goals for Everton

Dixie Dean	20

Everton hat tricks

Bertie Freeman	1909-10
Bobby Parker	1914-15
Dixie Dean	1928-29 } home &
Dixie Dean	1928-29 } away
Duncan Ferguson	1997-98

BRADFORD CITY

Head to head

| Home | Everton | Won 7 | Drew 5 | Lost 1 |
| Away | Everton | Won 4 | Drew 4 | Lost 5 |

Home
Bradford City's only win here was in the very first visit, in 1908-09, when they won 1-0. In the last Premiership meeting, in April 2001, Bradford missed 2 penalties.

Away
Everton have won one and drawn one of the 2 meetings in the Premiership.

Overall
Everton failed to win any of the first 6 games between the clubs, but in the last 16 meetings, Everton have lost just one.

Sent off
No one has been sent off in this fixture.

Most goals for Everton
Joe Clennell   5

Everton hat tricks
Joe Clennell   1919-20

CHARLTON ATHLETIC

Head to head

Home	Everton	Won 9	Drew 6	Lost 3
Away	Everton	Won 7	Drew 1	Lost 10

Home

Everton are unbeaten in the last 10 home games, their last defeat coming on 1 October 1949, when both sides finished in the bottom 5, but neither was relegated.

Away

Everton have lost twice in the last 8 visits to London against Charlton. Prior to the defeat at the Valley in December 2000, the last loss had been at Selhurst Park, in October 1986.

Overall

Everton have lost only twice in the last 17 meetings home and away, winning 7 of the last 8 games.

Sent off

At Goodison Park, on 21 March 1987, both Ian Snodin of Everton, and Andy Peake of Charlton, were sent off. At Goodison, in August 2000, Charlton's former Blue, Carl Tiler, received his marching orders.

Most goals for Everton
Dixie Dean   5

Everton hat tricks
Dixie Dean   1930-31

Most goals for Charlton
Jim Melrose   4

Charlton hat tricks
Jim Melrose   1986-87

CHELSEA

Head to head

Home	Everton	Won 33	Drew 19	Lost 10
Away	Everton	Won 12	Drew 19	Lost 31

Home

Since 1984, Everton have won just 5 of the 16 matches at Goodison, losing on 4 occasions.

Away

At Stamford Bridge, Everton's last win was in November 1994, with Paul Rideout grabbing the winner. The last 6 meetings have seen 3 draws and 3 defeats for the Blues.

Overall

Everton have won only 2 of the last 12 meetings home and away.

Sent off

At Stamford Bridge, on 12 October 1985, Kevin Ratcliffe memorably took over in goal when Neville Southall was sent off. Chelsea's last 2 visits to Goodison have seen Frank Leboeuf and Jimmy Floyd Hasselbaink receive their marching orders.

Most goals for Everton

Dixie Dean	10
Joe Royle	7
Roy Vernon	5

Everton hat tricks

Bertie Freeman	1908-09
S Fazackerley	1920-21
Dixie Dean	1931-32

Most goals for Chelsea

George Mills	9
Peter Osgood	8
George Hilsdon	7
Roy Bentley	7
Kerry Dixon	7
Jimmy Greaves	6

Chelsea hat tricks

George Hilsdon	1907-08
George Hilsdon	1908-09
George Mills	1936-37
Roy Bentley	1955-56
Gordon Davies	1984-85

COVENTRY CITY

Head to head

Home	Everton	Won 18	Drew 12	Lost 5
Away	Everton	Won 11	Drew 7	Lost 17

Home

Coventry have lost only twice in the last 10 games, in 1991-92 and 1998-99. The 1-1 draw, on the final day of the 1997-98 season, secured Everton's Premiership status.

Away

The 3-1 win at Highfield Road, in January 2001, was Everton's first win in 8 visits, since a Mark Ward goal settled the game in March 1993.

Overall

Everton have won only 3 of the 18 meetings in the Premiership.

Sent off

Marco Materazzi at Goodison, in April 1999, was the last sending-off in the fixture.

Most goals for Everton

Bob Latchford	10
Joe Royle	6
Graeme Sharp	6

Everton hat tricks

Bob Latchford	1977-78
Peter Beardsley	1991-92

Most goals for Coventry

Ian Wallace	7
Cyril Regis	5
Terry Gibson	4
Ernie Hunt	4

Coventry hat tricks

David Cross	1975-76
Jim Melrose	1982-83

DERBY COUNTY

Head to head

Home	Everton	Won 37	Drew 12	Lost 12
Away	Everton	Won 22	Drew 9	Lost 30

Home
In the last 17 games Derby have won only once, a 2-1 victory on 14 February 1998.

Away
Everton scored 6 goals at the old Baseball Ground on 3 occasions, the only instance in League history, on any ground, where the away side has achieved this feat. Since the fixture was moved to Pride Park, in 1997, the Blues have lost all 4 games.

Overall
In the last 30 League games, home and away, Derby have won only 6 times, but the recent form line shows Derby winning 5 of the last 8 meetings.

Sent off
In 1997-98, at Derby, Andy Hinchcliffe was dismissed, whilst Richard Dunne was sent off at Pride Park in August 1999.

Most goals for Everton

Dixie Dean	18
Fred Geary	10
Alex Latta	8
Edgar Chadwick	7

Everton hat tricks

A McKinnon	1888-89
T Wylie [4]	1890-91
Fred Geary	1892-93 } same
Alex Latta	1892-93 } game
J Peacock	1920-21
Dixie Dean	1928-29
Jimmy Cunliffe	1936-37
Eddie Wainwright	1953-54

Most goals for Derby County

Steve Bloomer	13
Jack Bowers	10
John Goodall	6

Derby County hat tricks

Jack Bowers	1931-32
Dai Astley	1936-37

FULHAM

Head to head

Home	Everton	Won 9	Drew 4	Lost 0
Away	Everton	Won 3	Drew 4	Lost 6

Home

Everton have won the last 8 meetings at Goodison, going back to 1959.

The meeting in the Premiership, in the 2001-02 season, will be the first since Everton won 5-1 at Goodison, on 21 May 1968, 3 days after the FA Cup Final defeat by West Bromwich Albion.

Away

Everton have won only 1 of the last 7 visits to Craven Cottage, the only victory being on the opening day of the season in 1966-67, when Alan Ball scored the only goal on his debut.

Overall

Of all the clubs in the Premiership, in the 2001-02 season, only Bolton Wanderers have a worse overall record than Fulham, in League games against Everton.

Most goals for Everton

Derek Temple   6

Everton hat tricks

Harry Catterick	1950-51
Roy Vernon	1962-63

IPSWICH TOWN

Head to head

Home	Everton	Won 11	Drew 11	Lost 3
Away	Everton	Won 9	Drew 6	Lost 10

Home

The 3-0 defeat, in September 2000, was Everton's first loss in 10 games at Goodison against Ipswich, since the infamous 4-0 defeat in February 1980.

Away

At Ipswich, Everton have lost only 2 in the last 6 away games.

Overall

Last season was the first time Ipswich had completed a 'double' of home and away wins against Everton in a season.

Sent off

Stuart Barlow, on 9 May 1995, and Alex Nyarko, on 24 February 2001, both at Portman Road, are the last 2 players sent off in the fixture.

Most goals for Everton

Joe Royle	6
Graeme Sharp	4

Everton hat tricks

Derek Temple	1961-62

Most goals for Ipswich Town

Paul Mariner	6
John Wark	5
Trevor Whymark	5
Eric Gates	4
Alan Brazil	4
Ray Crawford	4

Ipswich hat tricks

None

LEEDS UNITED

Head to head

Home	Everton	Won 22	Drew 16	Lost 11
Away	Everton	Won 3	Drew 11	Lost 35

Home

Everton are unbeaten at Goodison in the last 10 games, since losing 3-2 on the opening day of the 1990-91 season.

Away

Everton have gone 35 games without a win, which came in September 1951, in Division 2. The Blues have scored only 5 times in the last 17 visits. The last victory in the top-flight was in the Championship-winning year of 1938-39.

Sent off

In the 1-1 draw at Elland Road, in May 2000, 3 players were dismissed, Michael Duberry [Leeds], Richard Dunne and Don Hutchison [Everton].

Most goals for Everton

Dixie Dean	11
Bob Latchford	5

Everton hat tricks

Dixie Dean	1925-26
Robert 'Bunny' Bell	1938-39
Bob Latchford	1979-80

Most goals for Leeds

Peter Lorimer	6
Billy Bremner	6
Arthur Hydes	5
Johnny Giles	5
Mick Jones	5
Allan Clarke	5
Gordon Hodgson	5

Leeds hat tricks

Charlie Keetley	1928-29
Gordon Hodgson [4]	1937-38
Harry Brook	1956-57

LEICESTER CITY

Head to head

Home	Everton	Won 23	Drew 14	Lost 9
Away	Everton	Won 12	Drew 13	Lost 21

Home

The Blues 2-1 win, in February 2001, was preceded by 5 consecutive draws at Goodison between the teams. Everton's last win prior to 2001 had been a 5-1 victory on 28 December 1986.

Leicester's last victory was on 14 December 1985, when their 2-1 win featured a penalty by Gary McAllister.

Away

Everton have lost just one of the last 7 games at Filbert Street, since the defeat on the opening day of the 1985-86 campaign.

Overall

Leicester have won only once in the last 14 games home and away. The 2 League games in 1929-30, both ended in 5-4 wins for Leicester City.

Sent off

On 4 March 1995, Vinny Samways and Duncan Ferguson were both sent off at Filbert Street in a 2-2 draw.

Most goals for Everton

Dixie Dean	17
Tommy White	6
Bob Latchford	6

Everton hat tricks

Dixie Dean	1927-28
Dixie Dean [4]	1931-32
Dixie Dean	1932-33
Joe Royle	1968-69

Most goals for Leicester City

Arthur Chandler	9
Arthur Lochhead	6
Ernie Hine	6
Jimmy Walsh	6

Leicester City goals

Arthur Chandler	1929-30

MANCHESTER CITY

Head to head

Home	Everton	Won 35	Drew 19	Lost 15
Away	Everton	Won 14	Drew 17	Lost 38

Home
City have won only 2 of the last 11 games at Goodison.

Away
At Maine Road, Everton have won 4 of their last 20 visits, the 5-0 defeat in December 2000 was the Blues' biggest Premiership defeat.

Overall
Everton's last League 'double' over City was when they won both matches 2-0, in 1995-96, with Joe Parkinson scoring on each occasion. The last 16 games, home and away, have seen each side win 7 times with 2 draws.

Sent off
Both Alessandro Pistone [Everton] and Paul Dickov [Manchester City] were sent off in the clash at Goodison, in April 2001, although the latter's offence was later reduced to a yellow card.

Most goals for Everton

Alex Young [1901 – 1911]	9
Jack Taylor	7
Bobby Irvine	5
Alex Stevenson	5
Jimmy Harris	5

Everton hat tricks

Alex Young [4]	1906-07
Alex Young [4]	1908-09
Bobby Parker	1914-15
Wilf Chadwick	1923-24
Gary Lineker	1985-86

Most goals for Manchester City

Irvine Thornley	11
Tom Johnson	8
Tom Holford	7
Fred Tilson	7
Eric Brook	6

Manchester City hat tricks

Irvine Thornley	1907-08
Irvine Thornley	1908-0
Tom Holford	1908-09
Tom Holford [4]	1911-12
Tom Browell [4]	1925-26
Tom Johnson [5]	1928-29
Ken Barnes	1957-58

- Tom Johnson's 5-goal haul was the first against the Blues in League football, both he, and 4-goal Tom Browell, also played for Everton.

- All 3 of Ken Barnes' goals came from the penalty spot; the last instance in the top-flight in England.

MANCHESTER UNITED

Head to head

| Home | Everton | Won 36 | Drew 17 | Lost 19 |
| Away | Everton | Won 15 | Drew 18 | Lost 39 |

Home

United have won 5 and drawn 1 of the last 6 games and have lost only one in the last 11 encounters.

Away

Everton have recorded just one victory in the Premiership at Old Trafford, 3-0 in August 1992. Since then, United have won 7 and drawn 1 of the 8 matches.

Overall

The Blues have won only once in the last 17 meetings.

Sent off

David Unsworth was the last player sent off in the fixture, at Goodison, in September 1995.

Most goals for Everton

Graeme Sharp	10
Bobby Parker	9
Dixie Dean	7
Alex Young	6

Everton hat tricks

Alex Latta [4]	1892-93
Bobby Parker	1913-14
Stan Davies	1921-22
Dixie Dean [5]	1927-28

Most goals for Manchester United

Denis Law	8
Ole Gunnar Solskjaer	7
George Wall	6
Bobby Charlton	6
Lee Sharpe	5
Gordon Hill	5
Alex Dawson	5
Alex Turnbull	5

Manchester United hat tricks

Alex Dawson	1959-60
Ole Gunnar Solskjaer [4]	1999-00

• Bobby Charlton scored for United in the fixture in 3 different decades.

MIDDLESBROUGH

Head to head

Home	Everton	Won 33	Drew 10	Lost 5
Away	Everton	Won 13	Drew 13	Lost 22

Home

The 6 meetings in the Premiership have seen 2 wins apiece, Everton's being by 4-0, in 1995-96 and by 5-0, in 1998-99.

Away

Everton have won 3 of the 6 meetings in the Premiership.

Overall

Everton were undefeated in the fixture in 9 games between 1981 and 1995, but Middlesbrough have won 4 of the last 8 games.

Sent off

David Weir was the last Everton player sent off in the fixture, in October 1999. Alan Kernaghan, in April 1993, was the last Middlesbrough player dismissed.

Most goals for Everton

Tommy Lawton	9
Bob Latchford	8
Dixie Dean	8
Alex Young [1901 – 1911]	7

Everton hat tricks

J Brearley	1902-03
H Bolton	1906-07
Wilf Chadwick	1922-23
Jack Cock	1922-23
Tommy Lawton	1938-39 } home &
Tommy Lawton [4]	1938-39 } away

Most goals for Middlesbrough

George Camsell	8
Micky Fenton	6
Ralph Birkett	6

Middlesbrough hat tricks

Billy Birrell	1922-23
George Camsell [4]	1927-28
Ralph Birkett	1935-36
Alex McCrae	1950-51

NEWCASTLE UNITED

Head to head

Home	Everton	Won 36	Drew 13	Lost 18
Away	Everton	Won 16	Drew 15	Lost 36

Home

Since Newcastle returned to the top-flight under Kevin Keegan in 1993, they have won 3 times in their 8 visits to Goodison.

Away

Since winning 4-0 on Boxing Day, in 1986, the Blues have only won twice in the past 10 visits, in 1998-99 and 2000-01.

Overall

Everton have won only 5 of the last 17 games home and away, although they did do the 'double' in 1998-99.

Sent off

Slaven Bilic was the last to be sent off, at St James Park in September 1997. The last Newcastle player to be dismissed was Robert Lee, at Goodison in April 1995. Earlier that season there had been a dual sending-off of Barry Horne and Earl Barrett, at St James' Park.

Most goals for Everton

Dixie Dean	16
Tommy White	5
Alex Young [1901 – 1911]	5
Bob Latchford	5

Everton hat tricks

Dixie Dean	1925-26	} home & away
Dixie Dean	1925-26	
Dixie Dean	1928-29	
Bobby Collins	1960-61	
Wayne Clarke	1986-87	
Tony Cottee	1988-89	

Most goals for Newcastle

Hughie Gallagher	11
Tom McDonald	9
James Stewart	8
Alan Gowling	7

Newcastle hat tricks

Hughie Gallagher	1926-27
Len White	1959-60
Alan Gowling	1975-76

SOUTHAMPTON

Head to head

Home	Everton	Won 23	Drew 6	Lost 5
Away	Everton	Won 10	Drew 8	Lost 16

Home

Everton have lost only once in the last 9 games, and only twice in the last 23 games at Goodison.

Away

At The Dell, Southampton have won the last 4 games and are unbeaten in the last 7 meetings since 1994-95. In the 10 years prior to 1994-95, Everton had remained unbeaten, winning 7 games and drawing 3.

Overall

In the last 34 games, home and away, the Saints have won just 7 times.

Sent off

On March 7 1998, Slaven Bilic and Ken Monkou were both sent off at The Dell.

Most goals for Everton

Joe Royle	11
Graeme Sharp	6
Tony Cottee	6

Everton hat tricks

Joe Royle	1969-70
Joe Royle [4]	1971-72 } same
David Johnson	1971-72 } game
Gary Lineker	1985-86
Graeme Sharp [4]	1987-88
Gary Speed	1996-97

Most goals for Southampton

Mick Channon	6
Steve Moran	6
Ron Davies	5

Southampton hat tricks

None

● Everton have scored 8 goals, 7 goals and 6 goals in home matches against the Saints since 1970.

SUNDERLAND

Head to head

Home	Everton	Won 42	Drew 10	Lost 17
Away	Everton	Won 15	Drew 11	Lost 43

Home
Sunderland have won only once in the last 7 meetings, by 3-1 in November 1996.

Away
Everton have won only once in the last 9 visits, by 2-1, in 1984-85, when Derek Mountfield scored both goals.
Sunderland's last League game at Roker Park, on 3 May 1997, was a 3-0 win against Everton.

Sent off
The last 2 sendings-off have been Sunderland players at Goodison: Gordon Chisholm on Boxing Day 1983 and Don Hutchison on the final day of the 2000-01 season.

Most goals for Everton

Dixie Dean	16
Bobby Parker	8
Edgar Chadwick	7

Everton hat tricks

Edgar Chadwick	1893-94
Bertie Freeman	1908-09
Bobby Parker	1914-15
Dixie Dean [4]	1926-27
Tommy White	1929-30
Stan Bentham	1938-39
Eddie Wainwright	1946-47
Johnny Morrissey	1966-67

Most goals for Sunderland

Charlie Buchan	15
George Holley	12
Bob Gurney	11

Sunderland hat tricks

George Holley	1911-12
George Holley	1913-14
Robert Best	1913-14
Tommy Wright	1949-50

TOTTENHAM HOTSPUR

Head to head

Home	Everton	Won 29	Drew 21	Lost 14
Away	Everton	Won 13	Drew 19	Lost 32

Home

The Blues have won just once in 9 Premiership matches, by 1-0, in April 1997 – Spurs winning 4 times and drawing 4.

Away

Everton have not won in the last 15 League visits to White Hart Lane. Their last victory, in 1985-86, saw Gary Lineker score the winner.

Everton's only 3 wins, in the last 25 visits to Tottenham, came in consecutive seasons – 1983-84 and 1985-86.

In October 1958, Spurs inflicted upon Everton their biggest ever defeat, by 10-4.

Overall

Everton have won only once in the 18 Premiership games, with the Blues losing 10 and drawing 7.

Sent off

In September 1982, both John Lacy [Spurs] and John Bailey [Everton] were sent off in the clash at Goodison.

Most goals for Everton

Dixie Dean	9
Fred Pickering	7
Tony Cottee	7

Everton hat tricks

Joe Clennell	1914-15
Wilf Chadwick	1923-24
Dixie Dean	1934-35
Jimmy Harris	1958-59
Fred Pickering	1964-65
Tony Cottee	1991-92

Most goals for Tottenham

Bobby Smith	11
Martin Chivers	6
Chris Armstrong	6

Tottenham hat tricks

Eugene O'Callaghan [4]	1927-28
George Hunt	1933-34
Bobby Smith [4]	1958-59
Chris Armstrong	1998-99

● Both Smith and Harris scored hat tricks in the 10-4 game, in October 1958.

WEST HAM UNITED

Head to head

Home	Everton	Won 32	Drew 7	Lost 9
Away	Everton	Won 16	Drew 12	Lost 20

Home

West Ham have won twice in the last 11 games, with the Blues winning 6 consecutive matches until the 1-1 draw in November 2000.

Away

The Blues have lost just twice in the last 11 matches at Upton Park.

Overall

West Ham have won only 3 of the last 23 games, home and away, and only 7 of the last 42 matches.

Sent off

West Ham keeper, Ludek Miklosko, was dismissed at Goodison, in December 1995, and Stuart Pearce was sent off at Upton Park, on 31 March 2001.

Most goals for Everton

Dixie Dean	7
Roy Vernon	7
Derek Temple	6

Everton hat tricks

Dixie Dean	1931-32
Kevin Campbell	1998-99
Nick Barmby	1999-00

Most goals for West Ham

Vic Watson	7
Johnny Dick	6
Jimmy Ruffel	5

West Ham hat tricks

Vivian Gibbons	1928-29
Jimmy Ruffel	1931-32

Everton's other League opponents

What follows is a summary of the leading goalscorers and hat tricks in the fixtures with the club's other League opponents. Note that, unfortunately, there are no available records for some of the teams.

Most goals for Everton [where applicable]		Hat tricks [where applicable]	
Accrington Stanley			
Alf Milward	4		
Birmingham City			
Dixie Dean	11	Jack Southworth	1894-95
Bob Latchford	9	Alex Latta	1894-95
		Alf Milward	1895-96
		Jimmy Dunn	1931-32
		Dixie Dean	1935-36
		Alan Shackleton	1959-60
		Gary Lineker	1985-86
Blackpool			
Eddie Wainwright	7	Eddie Wainwright [4]	1948-49
Brentford			
Dave Hickson	5	Dave Hickson	1952-53
Bristol City			
Bertie Freeman	5	Andy King	1978-79
Burnley			
Dixie Dean	11	Edgar Chadwick	1890-91
		John Cameron	1896-97
		Dixie Dean	1925-26
		Dixie Dean [4]	1927-28
Bury			
Dixie Dean	9	None	
Alex Young [1901 – 1911]	7		
Bertie Freeman	7		
Cardiff City			
Dixie Dean	4	Bobby Collins	1960-61
		Roy Vernon	1961-62
Carlisle United			
Bob Latchford	2	None	
Crystal Palace			
Duncan Ferguson	4	Bob Latchford	1980-81
Darwen			
Jack Southworth	3	None	

Most goals for Everton		Hat tricks	
Doncaster Rovers			
Tommy Eglington	7	Tommy Eglington [5]	1952-53
Grimsby Town			
Dixie Dean	4	None	
Torry Gillick	3		
Huddersfield Town			
Dixie Dean	8	Sam Chedgzoy	1921-22
		Bobby Irvine	1921-22
		Dixie Dean	1931-22
		Jock Dodds	1947-48
		Eddie Wainwright	1949-50
Hull City			
John W Parker	4	John W Parker	1951-52
Luton Town			
John W Parker	6	None	
Graeme Sharp	6		
Millwall			
Kevin Sheedy	2	None	
Northampton Town			
Derek Temple	3	None	
Norwich City			
Mike Lyons	4	None	
Nottingham Forest			
Alex Young [1901 – 1911]	9	Jack Southworth	1894-95
Roy Vernon	7	Alex Young	1904-05
Graeme Sharp	6	Eddie Thomas	1959-60
John W Parker	6	Fred Pickering	1963-64
Jack Sharp	6		
Notts County			
Alex Latta	9	Alex Latta	1889-90
		Alex Latta	1891-92
		F Oliver	1905-06
		Bill Lacey	1910-11
		Adrian Heath	1983-84
Oldham Athletic			
John W Parker	5	Dixie Dean [4]	1930-31
		John W Parker	1953-54

Most goals for Everton		Hat tricks	
Plymouth Argyle			
Dixie Dean	4	Dixie Dean	1930-31
Jimmy Stein	4	Jimmy Stein	1930-31
		John W Parker [4]	1953-54
Portsmouth			
Dixie Dean	15	Dixie Dean	1927-28
		Dixie Dean	1928-29
		Dixie Dean	1929-30
		Tommy White	1931-32
		Alex Stevenson	1937-38
Preston North End			
Alf Milward	6	Jock Dodds	1948-49
		Eddie Thomas [4]	1957-58
Queens Park Rangers			
Bob Latchford	10	Bob Latchford [4]	1977-78
Graeme Sharp	6		
Rotherham			
Dave Hickson	4	John W Parker	1953-54
John W Parker	4		
Sheffield United			
Alex Young [1901 – 1911]	9	Edgar Chadwick	1895-96
Dixie Dean	8	Jack Sharp	1905-06
		Bertie Freeman	1908-09
		Bertie Freeman	1908-09
		Dixie Dean	1931-32
		Tony Cottee	1993-94
Sheffield Wednesday			
Dixie Dean	15	Jack Southworth [4]	1893-94
Jimmy Settle	7	Bertie Freeman	1909-10
Bobby Parker	7	Bobby Parker [4]	1914-15
Roy Vernon	7	Dixie Dean [5]	1931-32
		Alex Young	1965-66
		Andrei Kanchelskis	1995-96
Stoke City			
Fred Geary	8	Fred Geary	1889-90
Jack Taylor	7	T McInnes	1895-96
Dixie Dean	7	Dixie Dean	1930-31
		Jimmy Cunliffe [4]	1935-36
		Dave Hickson	1953-54

Most goals for Everton		Hat tricks	
Swansea			
Dixie Dean	4	None	
John W Parker	4		
Swindon Town			
Tony Cottee	3	Tony Cottee	1993-94
Watford			
Graeme Sharp	7	None	
Adrian Heath	6		
West Bromwich Albion			
Alan Ball	10	Alex Latta	1891-92
Jimmy Cunliffe	9	Jack Southworth [6]	1893-94
Dixie Dean	9	Jack Taylor	1896-97
John Bell	8	John Bell	1896-97
Jack Southworth	7	Jimmy Cunliffe [4]	1935-36
Jack Taylor	7	Dixie Dean	1936-37
		John Morrissey	1962-63
		Alan Ball	1967-68
		Alan Ball	1968-69
Wimbledon			
Kevin Sheedy	5	None	
Tony Cottee	4		
Wolverhampton Wanderers			
Joe Royle	10	A Hartley	1897-98
Fred Geary	8	Jimmy Settle	1901-02
		Jack Taylor	1901-02
		Jock Dodds	1947-48

Everton's other League opponents

Most goals against Everton [where applicable]		Hat tricks [where applicable]	
Birmingham City			
George Briggs	7	Noel Kinsey	1955-56
Peter Murphy	6	George Haywood	1932-33
George Haywood	6		
Blackpool			
Jackie Mudie	8	Dave Durie	1956-57
Stan Mortensen	7	Jackie Mudie	1955-56
Ray Charnley	6		
Brighton			
Michael Robinson	3	None	
Bristol City			
Sammy Gilligan	3	None	
Fred Staniforth	3		
Burnley			
Ray Pointer	8	Joe Anderson	1919-20
Brian Pilkington	5	Harry Potts	1949-50
John Connelly	5	Arthur Bellamy	1963-64
Carlisle United			
Frank Laidlow	3	None	
Grimsby Town			
Joe Robson	4	Joe Robson [4]	1929-30
Hull City			
Viggo Jensen	3	None	
Nottingham Forest			
Grenville Morris	6	Len Benbow	1898-99
Enoch West	6	John Calvey	1899-00
		Alfred Green	1907-08
Oldham Athletic			
Arthur Gee	10	None	
Queens Park Rangers			
Les Ferdinand	7	Andy Sinton	1992-93
		Les Ferdinand	1992-93
		Bradley Allen	1993-94

Most goals against Everton		Hat tricks	
Sheffield United			
Harry Johnson	10	Harry Hammond	1894-95
		George Brown	1906-07
		Harry Johnson [4]	1923-24
		Jack Wilkinson	1955-56
Sheffield Wednesday			
Ellis Rimmer	7	Andrew Wilson	1902-03
Mark Bright	6	Jimmy Trotter	1926-27
		Mark Hopper	1929-30
		Ellis Rimmer	1935-36
		Neil Dewar	1936-37
Stoke City			
Lee Chapman	3	None	
Watford			
John Barnes	3	None	
West Bromwich Albion			
Derek Kevan	15	Bobby Blood	1923-24
Jeff Astle	10	Derek Kevan [5]	1959-60
		Mickey Fudge	1963-64
Wimbledon			
John Fashanu	3	None	
Efan Ekoku	3		
Marcus Gayle	3		
Wolverhampton Wanderers			
Harry Wood	8	Gordon Clayton [4]	1936-37
Kenny Hibbitt	7	Dickie Dorsett	1938-39
Jimmy Murray	6	John Richards	1972-73

Most goals against Everton

Most League goals against Everton whilst playing for one club.

Charlie Buchan	15	Sunderland
Derek Kevan	15	West Bromwich Albion
Harry Hampton	14	Aston Villa
Steve Bloomer	13	Derby County
Ian Rush	13	Liverpool
George Holley	12	Sunderland
Ian Wright	12	Arsenal
Billy Walker	11	Aston Villa
Hughie Gallagher	11	Newcastle United
Bob Gurney	11	Sunderland
Irvine Thornley	11	Manchester City
Bobby Smith	11	Tottenham Hotspur
Harry Johnson	10	Sheffield United
Jeff Astle West	10	Bromwich Albion
Jack Bowers	10	Derby County
Charlie Gee	10	Oldham Athletic

- With 17 goals [15 for Sunderland and 2 for Arsenal], Charlie Buchan has scored more League goals against Everton than any other player.

- Steve Bloomer also scored twice for Middlesbrough, taking his overall total against the Blues to 15 goals.

Post-War career goals against Everton

Players who have scored 13 or more League goals against Everton in the post-War era.

15	Derek Kevan [West Bromwich Albion]
13	Ian Rush [Liverpool]
13	Ian Wright [12 for Arsenal, 1 for Crystal Palace]
13	Les Ferdinand [7 for QPR, 3 for Newcastle United, 3 for Tottenham]
13	David Herd [4 for Manchester United, 9 for Arsenal]

Regular post-War scorers against Everton

| 11 | Jimmy Greaves | 6 for Chelsea |
| | | 5 for Tottenham |

11	Alan Shearer	1 for Southampton
		7 for Blackburn
		3 for Newcastle United

10	Mark Bright	2 for Leicester City
		2 for Crystal Palace
		6 for Sheffield Wednesday

Players who have scored League goals against Everton for 4 different clubs

7	Gary McAllister	1 for Leicester City
		2 for Leeds United
		3 for Coventry City
		1 for Liverpool

4	Dean Saunders	1 for Oxford United
		1 for Derby County
		1 for Aston Villa
		1 for Liverpool

Notable players to score against Everton for 3 different clubs

7	George Graham	1 for Aston Villa
		3 for Chelsea
		3 for Arsenal

4	Teddy Sheringham	2 for Millwall
		1 for Tottenham
		1 for Manchester United

4	David Speedie	1 for Chelsea
		2 for Coventry City
		1 for Liverpool

Other scoring achievements against Everton

- Lee Chapman scored in the 3 major domestic competitions against Everton for different clubs: in the League for Stoke City and Leeds United, the FA Cup for Sheffield Wednesday and the League Cup for Leeds United.
- Billy Meredith scored 4 goals against the Blues for both Manchester City and United.

League record against other clubs

The following table shows Everton's playing record in League matches against other clubs. The teams are listed according to the success which the Blues have enjoyed in terms of the number of points won as a percentage of the total available [using 2 points for a win]. A success rate of less than 50% occurs when the Blues have won fewer games than the opposition.

	P	W	D	L	PTS	%
Northampton Town	2	2	0	0	4	100%
Reading	2	2	0	0	4	100%
Swansea City	12	8	4	0	20	83%
Watford	14	11	1	2	23	82%
Bradford	8	5	2	1	12	75%
Bristol Rovers	2	1	1	0	3	75%
Glossop	2	1	1	0	3	75%
Millwall	6	4	1	1	9	75%
Swindon Town	2	1	1	0	3	75%
Barnsley	8	4	3	1	11	69%
Brighton	8	4	3	1	11	69%
Bristol City	20	12	3	5	27	68%
Plymouth Argyle	6	4	0	2	8	67%
Notts County	66	37	13	16	87	66%
Accrington Stanley	10	5	3	2	13	65%
Birmingham City	104	54	27	23	135	65%
Grimsby Town	22	12	4	6	28	64%
Bolton Wanderers	116	59	27	30	145	63%
Darwen	4	2	1	1	5	63%
Fulham	26	12	8	6	32	62%
Stoke City	104	50	27	27	127	61%
Middlesbrough	96	46	23	27	115	60%
West Ham United	96	48	19	29	115	60%
Bradford City	26	11	9	6	31	60%
Southampton	68	33	14	21	80	59%
Oxford United	6	2	3	1	7	58%
Rotherham United	6	2	3	1	7	58%
Sheffield Wednesday	128	55	37	36	147	57%
Derby County	122	60	20	42	140	57%
Ipswich Town	50	20	17	13	57	57%
Wolverhampton W	114	54	20	40	128	56%
Burnley	98	41	28	29	110	56%
Bury	52	21	16	15	58	56%
Blackpool	46	20	11	15	51	55%
Coventry City	70	29	19	22	77	55%
Queens Park Rangers	42	18	10	14	46	55%

	P	W	D	L	PTS	%
Charlton Athletic	36	16	7	13	39	54%
Nottingham Forest	120	52	26	42	130	54%
Leicester City	92	35	27	30	97	53%
Luton Town	38	16	8	14	40	53%
Sheffield United	118	47	29	42	123	52%
Crystal Palace	24	9	7	8	25	52%
Wimbledon	28	9	11	8	29	52%
Preston North End	88	33	25	30	91	52%
Chelsea	124	45	38	41	128	52%
Norwich City	40	14	13	13	41	51%
West Bromwich Albion	132	52	31	49	135	51%
Huddersfield Town	56	22	13	21	57	51%
Blackburn Rovers	126	50	27	49	127	50%
Brentford	16	7	2	7	16	50%
Doncaster Rovers	6	2	2	2	6	50%
Hull City	6	3	0	3	6	50%
Leyton Orient	2	1	0	1	2	50%
Lincoln City	4	1	2	1	4	50%
Port Vale	2	1	0	1	2	50%
Aston Villa	172	64	42	66	170	49%
Newcastle United	134	52	28	54	132	49%
Sunderland	138	57	21	60	135	49%
Manchester City	138	49	36	53	134	49%
Liverpool	164	54	51	59	159	48%
Tottenham Hotspur	128	42	40	46	124	48%
Manchester United	144	51	35	58	137	48%
Cardiff City	30	10	8	12	28	47%
Oldham Athletic	28	9	8	11	26	46%
Portsmouth	44	16	8	20	40	45%
Arsenal	160	51	34	75	136	43%
Leeds United	98	25	27	46	77	39%
Carlisle United	2	0	0	2	0	0%

League record season by season

The club's League record is shown below. Seasons marked* are those spent in the 2nd Division.

			Home						Away				
	P	W	D	L	F	A	W	D	L	F	A	Points	Pos
1888-89	22	8	0	3	23	14	1	2	8	12	32	20	8
1889-90	22	8	2	1	40	15	6	1	4	25	25	31	2
1890-91	22	9	0	2	39	12	5	1	5	24	17	29	1
1891-92	26	8	2	3	32	22	4	2	7	17	27	28	5
1892-93	30	9	3	3	44	17	7	1	7	30	34	36	3
1893-94	30	11	1	3	63	23	4	2	9	27	34	33	6
1894-95	30	12	2	1	47	18	6	4	5	35	32	42	2
1895-96	30	10	4	1	40	17	6	3	6	26	26	39	3
1896-97	30	8	1	6	42	29	6	2	7	20	28	31	7
1897-98	30	11	3	1	33	12	2	6	7	15	27	35	4
1898-99	34	10	2	5	25	13	5	6	6	23	28	38	4
1899-00	34	11	1	5	30	15	2	6	9	17	34	33	11
1900-01	34	10	4	3	37	17	6	1	10	18	25	37	7
1901-02	34	11	2	4	31	11	6	5	6	22	24	41	2
1902-03	34	10	2	5	28	18	3	4	10	17	29	32	12
1903-04	34	13	0	4	36	12	6	5	6	23	20	43	3
1904-05	34	14	2	1	36	11	7	3	7	27	25	47	2
1905-06	38	12	1	6	44	30	3	6	10	26	36	37	11
1906-07	38	16	2	1	50	10	4	3	12	20	36	45	3
1907-08	38	11	4	4	34	24	4	2	13	24	40	36	11
1908-09	38	11	3	5	51	28	7	7	5	31	29	46	2
1909-10	38	8	6	5	30	28	8	2	9	21	28	40	10
1910-11	38	12	3	4	34	17	7	4	8	16	19	45	4
1911-12	38	13	5	1	29	12	7	1	11	17	30	46	2
1912-13	38	8	2	9	28	31	7	5	7	20	23	37	11
1913-14	38	8	7	4	32	18	4	4	11	14	37	35	15
1914-15	38	8	5	6	44	29	11	3	5	32	18	46	1
1919-20	42	8	6	7	42	29	4	8	9	27	39	38	16
1920-21	42	9	8	4	40	26	8	5	8	26	29	47	7
1921-22	42	10	7	4	42	22	2	5	14	15	33	36	20
1922-23	42	14	4	3	41	20	6	3	12	22	39	47	5
1923-24	42	13	7	1	43	18	5	6	10	19	35	49	7
1924-25	42	11	4	6	25	20	1	7	13	15	40	35	17
1925-26	42	9	9	3	42	26	3	9	9	30	44	42	11
1926-27	42	10	6	5	35	30	2	4	15	29	60	34	20
1927-28	42	11	8	2	60	28	9	5	7	42	38	53	1
1928-29	42	11	2	8	38	31	6	2	13	25	44	38	18
1929-30	42	6	7	8	48	46	6	4	11	32	46	35	22

	P	Home					Away					Points	Pos
		W	D	L	F	A	W	D	L	F	A		
1930-31	42	18	1	2	76	31	10	4	7	45	35	61	1
1931-32*	42	18	0	3	84	30	8	4	9	32	34	56	1
1932-33	42	13	6	2	54	24	3	3	15	27	50	41	11
1933-34	42	9	7	5	38	27	3	9	9	24	36	40	14
1934-35	42	14	5	2	64	32	2	7	12	25	56	44	8
1935-36	42	12	5	4	61	31	1	8	12	28	58	39	16
1936-37	42	12	7	2	56	23	2	2	17	25	55	37	17
1937-38	42	11	5	5	54	34	5	2	14	25	41	39	14
1938-39	42	17	3	1	60	18	10	2	9	28	34	59	1
1946-47	42	13	5	3	40	24	4	4	13	22	43	43	10
1947-48	42	10	2	9	30	26	7	4	10	22	40	40	14
1948-49	42	12	5	4	33	25	1	6	14	8	38	37	18
1949-50	42	6	8	7	24	20	4	6	11	18	46	34	18
1950-51	42	7	5	9	26	35	5	3	13	22	51	32	22
1951-52*	42	12	5	4	42	25	5	5	11	22	33	44	7
1952-53*	42	9	8	4	38	23	3	6	12	33	52	38	16
1953-54*	42	13	6	2	55	27	7	10	4	37	31	56	2
1954-55	42	9	6	6	32	24	7	4	10	30	44	42	11
1955-56	42	11	5	5	37	29	4	5	12	18	40	40	15
1956-57	42	10	5	6	34	28	4	5	12	27	51	38	15
1957-58	42	5	9	7	34	35	8	2	11	31	40	37	16
1958-59	42	11	3	7	39	38	6	1	14	32	49	38	16
1959-60	42	13	3	5	50	20	0	8	13	23	58	37	16
1960-61	42	13	4	4	47	23	9	2	10	40	46	50	5
1961-62	42	17	2	2	64	21	3	9	9	24	33	51	4
1962-63	42	14	7	0	48	17	11	4	6	36	25	61	1
1963-64	42	14	4	3	53	26	7	6	8	31	38	52	3
1964-65	42	9	10	2	37	22	8	5	8	32	38	49	4
1965-66	42	12	6	3	39	19	3	5	13	17	43	41	11
1966-67	42	11	4	6	39	22	8	6	7	26	24	48	6
1967-68	42	18	1	2	43	13	5	5	11	24	27	52	5
1968-69	42	14	5	2	43	10	7	10	4	34	26	57	3
1969-70	42	17	3	1	46	19	12	5	4	26	15	66	1
1970-71	42	10	7	4	32	16	2	6	13	22	44	37	14
1971-72	42	8	9	4	28	17	1	9	11	9	31	36	15
1972-73	42	9	5	7	27	21	4	6	11	14	28	37	17
1973-74	42	12	7	2	29	14	4	5	12	21	34	44	7
1974-75	42	10	9	2	33	19	6	9	6	23	23	50	4
1975-76	42	10	7	4	37	24	5	5	11	23	42	42	11
1976-77	42	9	7	5	35	24	5	7	9	27	40	42	9
1977-78	42	14	4	3	47	22	8	7	6	29	23	55	3
1978-79	42	12	7	2	32	17	5	10	6	20	23	51	4
1979-80	42	7	7	7	28	25	2	10	9	15	26	35	19

	Home						Away					Points	Pos
	P	W	D	L	F	A	W	D	L	F	A		
1980-81	42	8	6	7	32	25	5	4	12	23	33	36	15
1981-82	42	11	7	3	33	21	6	6	9	23	29	64	8
1982-83	42	13	6	2	43	19	5	4	12	23	29	64	7
1983-84	42	9	9	3	21	12	7	5	9	23	30	62	7
1984-85	42	16	3	2	58	17	12	3	6	30	26	90	1
1985-86	42	16	3	2	54	18	10	5	6	33	23	86	2
1986-87	42	16	4	1	49	11	10	4	7	27	20	86	1
1987-88	40	14	4	2	34	11	5	9	6	19	16	70	4
1988-89	38	10	7	2	33	18	4	5	10	17	27	54	8
1989-90	38	14	3	2	40	16	3	5	11	17	30	59	6
1990-91	38	9	5	5	26	15	4	7	8	24	31	51	9
1991-92	42	8	8	5	28	19	5	6	10	24	32	53	12
1992-93	42	7	6	8	26	27	8	2	11	27	28	53	13
1993-94	42	8	4	9	26	30	4	4	13	16	33	44	17
1994-95	42	8	9	4	31	23	3	8	10	13	28	50	15
1995-96	38	10	5	4	35	19	7	5	7	29	25	61	6
1996-97	38	7	4	8	24	22	3	8	8	20	35	42	15
1997-98	38	7	5	7	25	27	2	8	9	16	29	40	17
1998-99	38	6	8	5	22	12	5	2	12	20	35	43	14
1999-00	38	7	9	3	36	21	5	5	9	23	28	50	13
2000-01	38	6	8	5	29	27	5	1	13	16	32	42	16

Signed limited edition prints of the legends of sport and great sporting moments

All bigbluetube prints are strictly limited to 500 copies and are personally signed by the featured sportsmen. These two Everton prints are just two from our unrivalled selection.

[BBT048] **Legends Series** Alex Young scores for Everton, against Blackburn Rovers in 1961. Signed by Alex Young £25

[BBT036] **Cup Kings Series** FA Cup Final, Wembley 1966, 1984 and 1995. Three of Everton's victorious FA Cup winning captains. **Signed by Brian Labone, Kevin Ratcliffe and Dave Watson** £35